Art
&
Soul

Jim Hodges

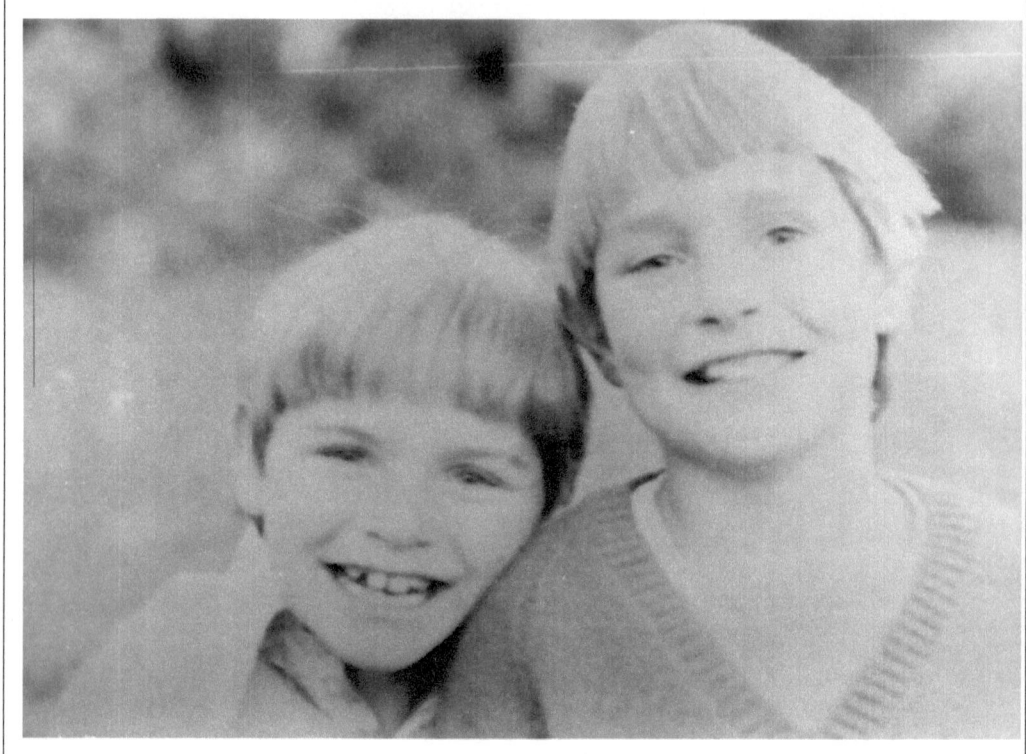

For Lee

Forward

I was born in England in 1965, though due to work opportunities offered to my father I spent most of my childhood growing up on the South Island of New Zealand. When my parents divorced I was 14 and I moved to Australia with my mother and only sibling—my brother Lee.

In 1982, the day before my 17th birthday, I joined the Royal Australian Navy and began a career which would span the next 23 years. Throughout the first 10 years of my career I bounced in and out of relationships and spent most of my free time pursuing women, parties and any rush I could find on my motorcycle. During those and subsequent years life dished up the trials and challenges most of us have to face, and through the influence of many people, places and experiences I began to discover myself.

I wrote my first poem in 1989 while serving on a Darwin-based patrol boat, simply to vent my frustrations at having to spend so many long nights at sea. Over the years my motives for writing a book have changed, and for many reasons the dream to get a book published never progressed any further than that—just a dream.

In 1992 I met my future wife, Vicky, and although the first few years of our relationship were at times volatile, we managed to struggle through it. Eventually two people who simply shared a bed became best friends and fell deeply in love.

In 1996 our daughter Ayeesha was born, followed eighteen months later by my son Bowie; and for a short time life seemed complete. Unfortunately, the truth was somewhat different, because beneath the surface lay a problem which had influenced most of my adult life; and this influence was becoming all-consuming.

On the 25th February 2001, I came to the realisation that my drinking had reached a stage where it was not only destroying my relationship with Vicky and the children, it had also begun jeopardising my career. I then made what I considered to be the hardest decision of my life, and placed myself in an alcohol rehabilitation program.

By June of that year I had accepted that I was an alcoholic and had begun my life of recovery. As for that difficult decision to do something about my drinking—well, it turned out to be the greatest decision I have ever, and probably ever will, make.

The complexities of sobriety are challenging, as are the complexities involved in simply living! However, sobriety has given me opportunities and rewards beyond anything I would have ever thought possible while I was drinking. In addition to the exceptional and complete life I now share with my family, I have set and accomplished many goals—not least of which has been finishing this book.

The following pages represent a cross section of my poems, thoughts and art; a view of the people I have encountered, the world I have seen, and a look at myself, stretching back to 1989, when I wrote my first verse.

Through my words and my art I have been able to give a gift to my brother, a memory to my children and theirs, a 'thank you' to my wife and my parents, but above all—I have realised a dream.

I hope that somewhere in these pages you find the inspiration to pursue or rekindle whatever dream you have or may have had at some point in your life. I truly believe that a life without dreams is a life only half-lived, and every person deserves to be all that they can be.

In no particular order—welcome to me!!!

J.H.

I believe –

Dreams are the substance of life.

Look to this day,
For it is life,
The very life of life.
In its brief course lie all
The realities and verities of existence,
The bliss of growth,
The splendour of action,
The glory of power-

For yesterday is but a dream,
And tomorrow is only a vision,
But today, well lived,
Makes every yesterday a dream of happiness
And every tomorrow a vision of hope.

Look well, therefore, to this day.

Sanskrit proverb
By Kalidasa,
Indian poet and playwright,
Fourth century A.D.

I BELIEVE

As the downpour of days becomes years,
Familiarity and surrender too easily take hold,
Blotting vision and suffocating passion.
To transcend fear and once again explore living
Is to leap to the heavens, breathe freedom
And again, continue to grow.

Searching

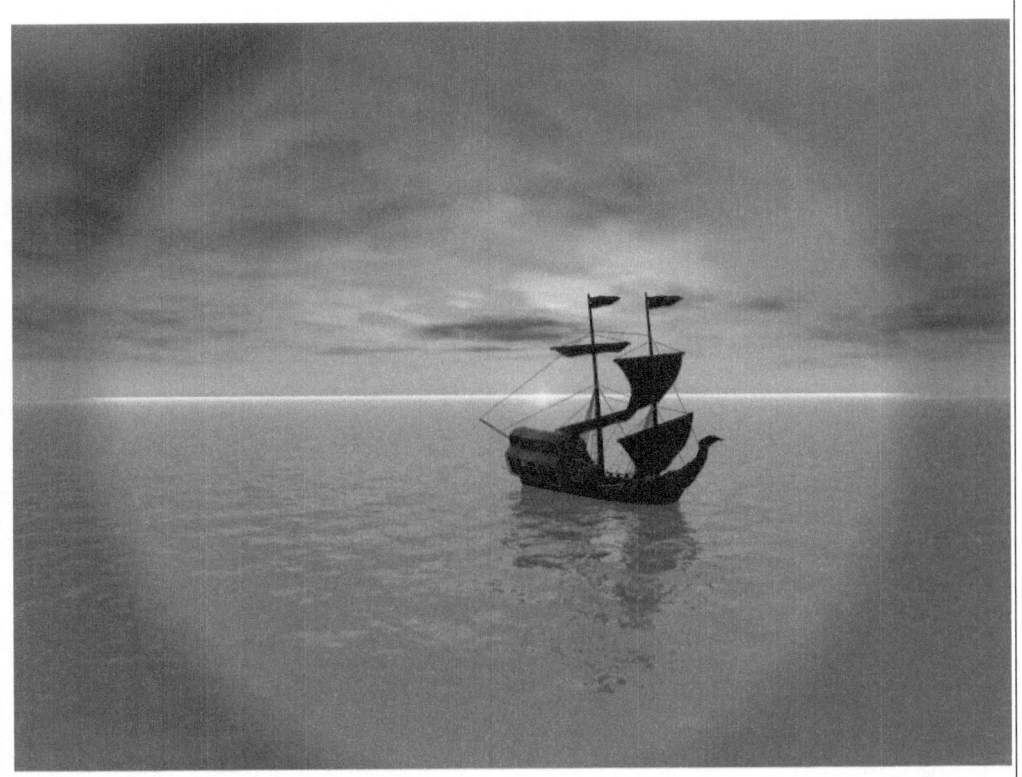

I BELIEVE

The freshness of new life breeds hope,
Instils passion and brings light to shadows.
The circle of life turns, connecting us all
To a greater purpose than individualism,
A greater destiny than self,
And will ultimately unite humanity.

Mighty Lady

A warship never sleeps, never tires, never weeps;
But lives and breathes with the life of the present,
Pulsating with the souls of a distant past,
Her heartbeat and her voice a constant companion
To those who served before and to those who will again.
She is a mystery, an enigma, a challenge —
She is many things to many men.

A tired mistress who requires painful attention;
One who demands respect, dictates loyalty and commitment.
To those who serve, her thanks and repayment in kind
Is that of drudgery — long days and empty nights
Of loneliness, absence and weary confinement.
Unforgivingly harsh and a true task master,
She is a tired mistress who will give no quarter.

A beautiful lady, who shines through trials and tribulations;
Keeper and protector of righteousness,
Of value, moral standards and ideals.
A symbol of nations; a wonder to behold.
She exemplifies honour and typifies pride;
A chariot, a conduit for faith and hope.
A beautiful lady who encompasses all things noble.

Her life-blood — sailors — give her magnificence,
Each with their own unique manner and character.
The different creeds, beliefs, ideals and histories
Thrust together, meld and bond as one,
With a single goal, purpose and direction —
To ensure that she breathes, to achieve
The greatness that destiny has bestowed upon her.

She has been, and will be, many things to many men,
But for me she stirs consciousness and conflicting memories.
She has been my home, my prison—a sanctuary, a trap;
The source of joy and pain, of passion and anguish.
I know I will never escape her profound impact or her hold,
For years with her have moulded perceptions,
Have etched changes within my heart and upon my soul.

I will always be overwhelmed by a surge of affection
Each time I reflect upon that brief moment in time
When my service was dedicated to her life.
The tides of change will never dull or wash away
Those years of bittersweet memories,
And my heart will always resonate with mixed emotion
As I look back at her from destiny's distant path.

So when she wreaks vengeance with feminine wrath
Or you feel the sting of her unforgiving demeanour,
Remember what it is to sail within her;
What it means to be a part of that life-blood.
Take pride; take comfort and solace from the knowledge
It was your commitment, your strength and your passion
That gave spirit to a Mighty Lady of the Sea.

Monsoon at Sea

Like phosphorus, glowing, aquatic plankton bright,
The waves are silvered within lightning's night.
A moon so full, another storm moves in,
A horizon dark like the blackest sin.

Shimmering shapes caress the sky of night,
The cold atmosphere now grips me tight.
A drop of rain passes down my chin;
The first of many, the monsoon will win.

Distorted figures within the clouds so bleak,
Overbearing giants search for the weak.
Starlight dreams succumb to the storm,
Churning seas blend without real form.

Curling winds howl, like wolves who seek
The long forgotten, the old or the meek.
A monsoon is beauty, yet full of scorn
For it knows no mercy—it will not mourn.

A silver fork again strikes the sea;
It's a stark reminder of what will be.
Nature's cry is a thunderous crash;
Sky black with grey, like pitch and ash.

City lights afar, it is sanctuary;
Yet on an ocean so fierce they won't save me.
Icy fingers of air begin to thrash,
Against our boat's side waves now crash.

Towards the earth drenching raindrops pour,
I think of the warm haven upon the shore.
Methodical drums, it's the seas own beat;
The sky fills again with a silver sheet.

A chill now stalks me down to my core,
Though the cold and wet I try to ignore.
For daring to sail, this fate I'll meet,
For when you face Mother Nature, you cannot cheat.

Foaming waters rise, they gush and tear.
I must fight the fear, must grin and bear.
Nature's anger is what I have met,
But it will pass, on this I'll bet.

I have survived the fear and seen the might,
Lived to tell of that distant night.
Between the wind and rain, the cold and wet,
A monsoon at sea, you will never forget.

Viking Gods

Viking Gods—speak to me
Whilst Neptune shows his might,
Wreaking havoc within a warring season
This cold, most southern night.
I feel a prickling within my soul
Stirring deep thoughts of lonely dread,
Praising soldiers of the sea—
Sailors long since dead

Viking Gods—save our souls
As Neptune displays his wrath,
And bring to us calm waters near
By wielding your mighty staff.
The wind it screams like dying dogs
Through modern iron mast,
In life's plot, to serve the seas
We sailors have been cast.

Viking Gods—crush this storm
Stirred by the old man of the sea,
And from these tides that clutch us tight
Give us the strength to break free.
Deliver us from fear of death,
The might of evil's grip
And bring us peace from what consumes
Our hearts, our minds, our ship.

Viking Gods—we've served you true
Upon this ocean's stage,
So often have we danced this song
To appease this awful rage.
But if fate is cruel and destiny bestows
An untimely watery grave,
For all the loves we left behind
We ask our souls you save.

Many Gods—many prayers,
Many nations' sailing men.
Like those before and those to come
We will triumph once again.
And so a future may come to pass
When we remember our southern plight,
And we will give thanks to a gracious God
Who saw us through that night.

Warship Away

With solitude for walls
And drab grey as my companion
I eke out an existence,
Forever mindful of my goals—
Painfully aware of my circumstance,
Showing no resistance—
Just necessity to strive and to succeed.

It is by my own choosing, this isolation,
From a society drowning in hypocrisy,
Weaned in an era of pompous arrogance.
Should this life be my conduit, my vehicle
To happiness and contentment?
But for it, I bleed.

This stepping stone
Laughing irony dictates
I must first serve—to be, to see
A way ahead; a path, a future—
One which envelopes all I love:
One that caresses my life entirely.

How do I weigh the cost?
To miss my child's changing face;
The warm embrace, smile and goodnight kiss.
Each year passing quicker than the last,
I can't return to pick up lost memories
Of those precious moments missed.

My sacrifice, the bed I made,
I shall not wish my life away.
Just stay and do my time,
For the end result is what I chase.
The bigger picture is what I see—
Once released, remaining days so free.

And rather than regret missed chances
Or dwell on lost opportunity,
I shall embrace life, love and family
With more vigour, more passion
Than I had ever known possible.
A warship away, another day.

Lonely

Red, yellow, orange, purple and white
A blending of colours, the dawning of night.
The sun melts away as my mind goes to wander—
A day's beautiful demise, about us I will ponder.

But by being reminded, she plays on my mind—
Fate and its fortunes are often unkind.
We joined our lives so together we'd be,
But a sailor is also wed to the sea

The sea is our home but it takes second place
To the warmth of her touch, the smile on her face.
How lonely our hearts get for that one soul.
She is left behind, will it take its toll?

We have loved before and lost in the past,
Creeping thoughts in the mind, will this one last?
We think of our loved ones and dream but why
Loneliness consumes like the distant night sky.

The moon and the stars are glistening like charms
But they hold no pleasure when I'm not in her arms.
The wind and the waves, nature she cries
Just to be with her now, beheld in her eyes.

The nights become longer, thoughts start to drift.
On watch alone, through memories I sift.
Will she be there when I return this time?
Getting so far was an uphill climb.

A thousand thoughts within, paranoia takes hold.
When I get home, will she be cold?
I have to trust what I know to be true;
That our love is strong, these times we'll get through.

Loneliness—the tide that sweeps through our being.
Without us as one, life has no meaning.
Our lives aren't so different, we share what we can,
But with my being away, it's the future we plan.

Remembering the vows, until death do us part;
Though we aren't together, she lays in my heart.
They say absence makes the heart grow fonder,
Constantly away, can I take this much longer?

We all hide our feelings in a different way,
She will ask, "Please, why won't you stay?"
By the look in her eyes, separation's my sin
But she knows that my feelings are hiding within.

Like the changing weather, so flows my mind.
I sink with the thought of her left behind,
For being alone is a pain too great—
It slowly consumes as we walk toward fate.

To know love's returned unconditionally
Is to appreciate a life that remains truly free.
There's no greater feeling than to mutually care
And to know that together, both lives you will share

To others we're numbers, just cabs off the rank,
But a lonely heart has no-one to thank.
We will work our long days and do it with ease,
For when we get home it's our loves we shall please.

Reflections

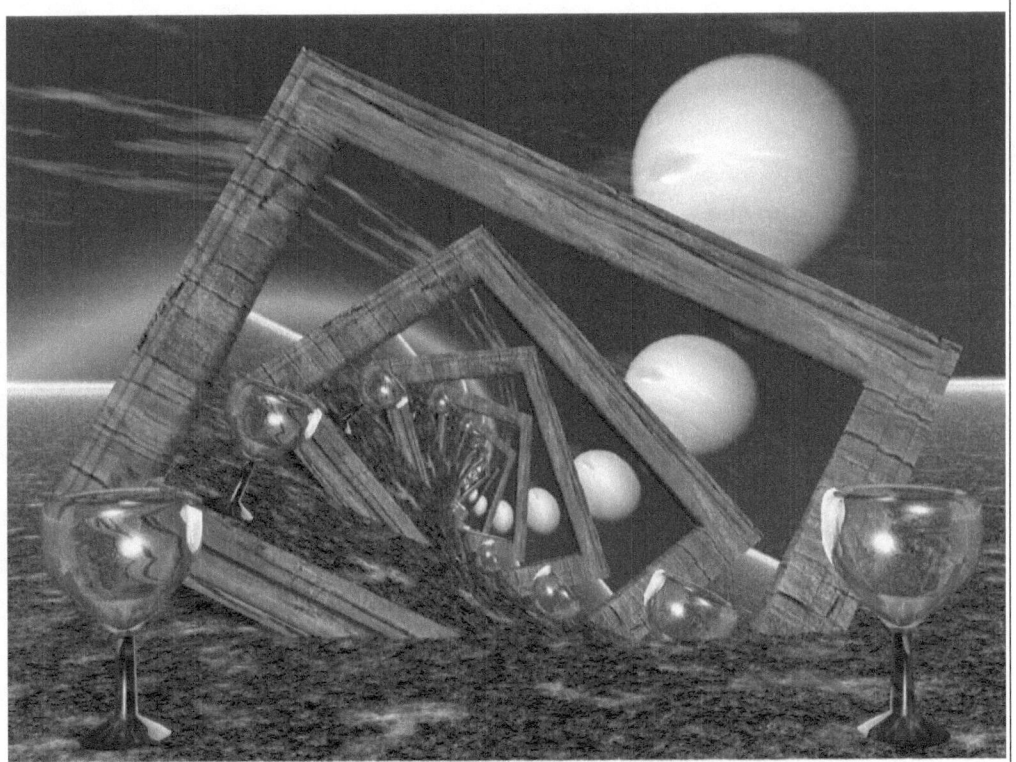

I BELIEVE

Within the abstract nature of ourselves,
Untold mysteries lay hidden, and beg unfolding and exploration.
To embrace the challenge and truth of our inner being
Is to begin a spiritual journey
And release the power of all our dreams.

Lessons

Life—the grand master, mentor and parent
Teaching lessons that can never be fully learnt.
So cruel these lessons, leaving more questions than answers—
Teasing, tantalizing, frustrating
And yet begging addiction.

A folly, an empty pursuit, a race?
All men are destined to chase, destined to pursue.
Some will attain great heights,
Others will falter, fall by the wayside.
Who will I be? What will I learn?

How am I to become the parent I know I should be?
How am I to become a teacher and mentor
To those that I hold most precious and dear—
My children, my future, my innocent babies.
Is it possible for me to impart all that I should?

Goodness, love, compassion and truth?
Can I possibly do justice to their innocence,
Their naivety and love for me?
Knowing my own lessons are only partially learnt,
Understanding that life has much to teach.

Can I transcend my own fears and confusions?
Is the knowledge and wisdom I've acquired enough?
Less answers, more questions, life dealing more cards—
Has the hand I have been dealt amply equipped,
Amply prepared and laid out my path?

A path of righteousness and honesty within my heart.
Will I be able to, without prejudice or bias,
Instil ideals; enlighten my children, helping them grow
To mature, blossom and flower
Into all they should be, can be, will be?

Are my concerns unfounded, without merit?
Do I dwell on mistakes, faults and evils
Which never may come to pass, never eventuate?
Or is life again teasing, tormenting?
A mind uncertain, one new to fatherhood.

I wonder was my father burdened with these questions.
Were his strengths and weaknesses imparted to me?
And was his guidance, teachings and love an easy task?
The fact that I can ask these questions
Supposes he succeeded; suggests maybe
Caring and love provide their own answers.

So it is with life, with love—becoming a dad.
Distant questions, unseen direction, uncertain future,
Yet I know within my heart of hearts
That as much as I need to achieve all that is right
I will falter and continue to spend my life learning.

In truth, perfection is an impossible task.
There are no firm rules, no right or wrongs.
For our children, as individuals, will grasp life
As we did, as we do—but in their own unique way;
Tasting, feeling and touching with their own minds.

To ponder these questions is but a small step,
For some answers already lie within my heart.
I must impart life's lessons, values, ideals and truths;
Breathe good and honest life into my babies, my immortality.
There is but one lesson for my children and for me.

Success rarely arrives easily
And failure is not a measure of the end result;
With that I can not, will not and shall not fail
As every ounce of energy, every moment of love
I will dedicate to being a good dad.

The Spark

Contemplating the embers of what once had been
A thought of smouldering romance,
I realised that the flames of a past
Were only in need of rekindling,
Of stoking and stirring
To be revived with a breath of fresh air.

Before the unbridled passion of making love
We must first find the reason we fell in love
Before honesty, trust and commitment dissolve.
We must resolve differences, destroy the barriers
Before broken hearts set like stone.
We must recover that which drew our souls together.

We must begin a journey of rediscovery—
One which can only be started through forgiveness.
We must discover the past that joined us as one
And soften the jaws of anger and bitterness.
We must dance with truth and embrace its warmth
Then sleep with belief and faith.

We must recapture the spirit
Of the destiny that drew us together.
We must give consciousness to our true heart
And share all that torments, all that invigorates.
We must grasp with both hands our mortality
And realise we have no time to waste.

We will return to the paradise we once embraced
Then travel to a perfection far beyond.
But to achieve what we must and find what we seek
We will have to endure the hardships of life, of love.
Sacrifice, uncertainty, atonement—
That will be our penance, the price of devotion.

For me, my journey must begin with a promise—
A promise which flows deep from my heart.
A promise to love, to protect and cherish
Your soul, your heart, your being;
A commitment of dedication and loyalty
To you and only you, eternally.

These are the things which will provide the spark,
Rekindle a most passionate affair.
Like bellows they will fan a fire
So bright, so fierce it will light a lifetime;
Inflame, engulf two hearts and two souls
For an eternity of loving contentment.

I believe –

The sins of the father don't have to be revisited.

Dream

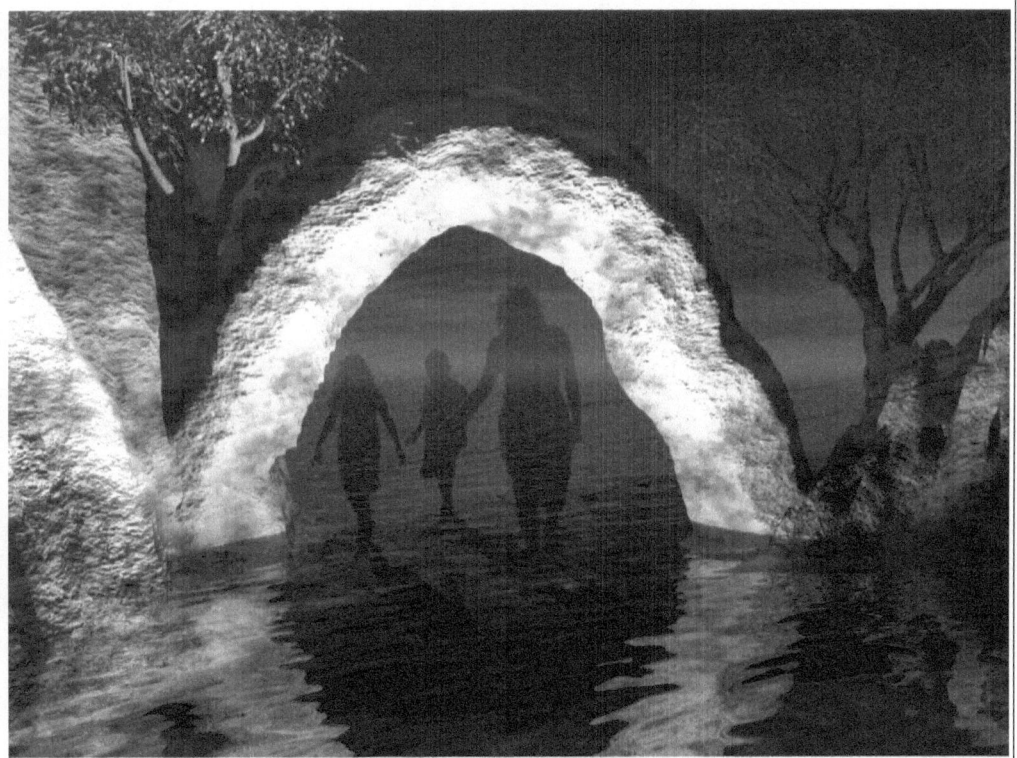

I believe –

In the absolute power of love.

Missing Home

It is a miracle: the time I have to share,
To be blessed with more love than one man deserves,
To feel the pulse of life within me
And be able to embrace all that is granted.
Although circumstance dictates that all I hold most precious
Should be placed out of physical reach,
I find solace and inspiration in the wonders nature provides—
A sunset, the stars, the sea and the breeze;
These things bring my heart back to you,
Bring me closer in spirit to all that I miss.

My first-born child, my beautiful daughter and apple of my eye,
With her unspoiled innocence and personality that lights a room;
Her cheeky smile as she says, "I love you, Daddy",
Without possibly knowing how deeply she touches my heart;
The tears in her eyes when she knows she has done wrong,
Followed by a "Sorry" and the warmest of cuddles;
The innocent look when tormenting her little brother,
Revealing her vindictive streak, testing her bounds,
Then showing compassion when he is sick or upset,
Pampering and smothering him with the most beautiful affection.

An imagination so naively perfect, untouched by the world—
Sharing imaginary tea with invisible friends,
Playing horse rides, hide 'n' seek and wrestling.
Just to see her eyes sparkle as we immerse ourselves in fun,
To walk together holding hands as she gazes admiringly my way
And feel that tight grip as she tries to keep pace.
To hear those words, "*Another* story, Daddy"
As I turn the last page of the second book,
And then to play her nightly bed time game—
This doll, that doll, more books and Mr Music Man.

My first born son, my own little man,
Still unable to speak a word
Yet his enormous smile and contagious giggle
Speak louder than all the words in the world.
The way he tries to walk with a total look of determination,
Only to be crawling again thirty-seconds later
With a grin that says, "It is much easier this way."
To watch him admiring his sister and dote on her every move—
Chasing, playing, loving every ounce of attention she pays him
While filling my every being with unimaginable joy.

To hold him in my arms and caress his tiny body
And watch him as he peacefully sleeps in childlike slumber,
Feeling his little heartbeat and the warmth of his face
Before going to bed, putting my mind at ease.
To laugh with him as he pats the cat, pulling clumps of fur,
Not knowing his own strength, and just learning to be gentle.
Playing in the bath; splashing, squirting, just loving the water;
Making castles from bubbles then blowing them down.
To experience the simple things, like watching him eat—
Just to see my boy growing and changing each minute, each day.

My best friend, confidante and partner
With whom all my secrets, frustrations and loves are shared.
To hold and take strength from her in moments of doubt
And soar to new and great heights as dreams are fulfilled.
Just to share all the joys and gifts which fill our lives—
My lover, and one true passion.
To smell her body and hair as we snuggle at night,
And to listen to her breathe and sigh whilst sleeping contently,
While watching her eyes flicker in faraway dreams.
To make love and be loved: feeling, tasting, touching perfection.

To be with the woman who raises my children—
Guiding, teaching, loving and protecting them.
To be able to show her how much I care,
How much I appreciate all that she does and all that she is.
To be constantly able to experience her gentleness:
The way she slides her hand through my hair as she passes me by
And tenderly kisses me at the end of a long day.
Just to see her smile and hear her laugh—
To be a part of all the things that her make whole.

These are but a few of life's gifts that make my heart ache
When not able to share each moment, each treasure.
But each star shines with the light of their eyes,
So every night as I gaze toward the heavens I am with them.
Each sunrise brings the warmth and beauty of family close.
The start of a new day and my heart is home where it belongs.
The breeze in the air, the breath of life
Reminding me of all that I cherish; all that is truly important
And how it is but a small drop in time that I should be away.
Within my mind, nature provides what absence steals.

Eyes Of My Children

Somewhere I lost my way, lost my focus, my direction;
Faded into all that I once despised and loathed,
Became that which I promised I would not.
The exact moment in time, the defining event,
So distant that it too lies unknown—
Buried in the mass of the past, hidden in a blur,
A sea of a thousand memories, decisions and mistakes.

When did the eyes of youth suddenly close?
Or was the vision eroded so slowly
It was impossible to see the change?
Whatever, whenever the reason, the cause
I know but one thought; feel but one pain—
That of loss, begot by innocence forever stained
By life, by experience; through pleasure and suffering.

For pieces of silver I have sold my soul,
For the satisfaction of flesh I sacrificed dignity and honour.
How long must I endure this feeling of scorn or disdain
For myself, my fellow man and our selfish pursuits?
Will I taste once again the pleasure of compassion
Or the delight of faith, hope and love?
Or am I destined to suffer this endless torment?

Has cynicism and pessimism clouded and consumed
All that I once believed, infected all that once was good
To a point where I am beyond redemption,
Enduring this tortured path, spent with malice.
Why must living dictate that all things pure
Eventually become soured, blackened by time?
And why must the price of wisdom and enlightenment
Be so high?

Will there ever be another day when I can gaze
Content at my own reflection and the reflections of others
Without feeling the bite, the sting of contempt?
Will my mortality achieve a single great purpose?
Has destiny set a course? Has fate or God decreed
That my soul's emptiness once again will flourish
With direction, purpose and youthful clarity?

These questions, these feelings, this deluded paradigm
For all too long preoccupied a dying soul
Drowning all in an ocean of self-pity and confusion.
I became content to lie in apathetic excuse,
Content to breathe in the vapour of excess.
So I remained ignorant, blind to the knowledge
That salvation and deliverance lay but a whisper away.

My defining moment came with the birth of my babies—
This miracle of life, so powerful, so wonderful.
And the beauty of this world and the joy of living
Became again the focus of my vision.
For my seeds are the beginning of a fresh tomorrow,
The continuation of another's hopeful yesterday—
The dreams and fancies of an unknown's future.

The eyes of my children lifted the veil and cleared the haze,
For they hold within them the key, the light.
Pure of heart, pure of thought, so beautifully perfect;
For within them I see myself, my children's children,
With their doubt, their pains, loves and lives yet to come
I see a future where they play a part
In man's quest for humanity, harmony
... as I now play mine.

But for today, this moment, they have brought to life
Hope, expectation, optimism and love.
They have given breath, given substance
To an existence frayed and dull.
They have filled a man's heart with a most wondrous faith,
A faith that has for so long been absent—
A faith in future, in charity of spirit, in mankind.

They have given birth to a soul invigorated by love,
Enriched a life far beyond the realms of imagination.
They have filled a mind with devotion and passion,
Rescued a spirit drifting and lost.
They have given freely, unknowingly, innocently.
And so to them I give a lifetime of love and dedication,
For the eyes of my children have rescued a heart.

Thought

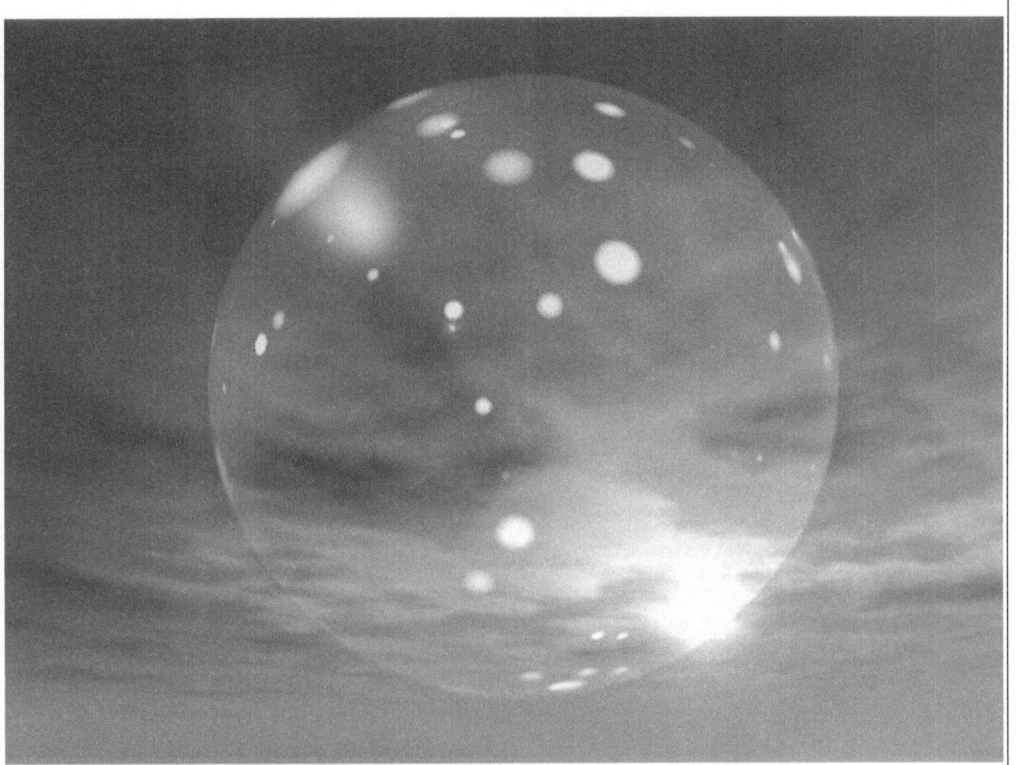

I believe –

Each new day is a fresh beginning

Lost Thoughts

Trying to find inspiration
So quiet
Country quiet, not man-made bustle
The log fire crackles
My thoughts drift to you
Dreaming
Gleaming

Waves crash upon winter's beach
Cast aside dreams, out of reach
Yet wind thrashes through autumn leaves
Alone in my tin shed
Is this what I'd hoped for?
Is this what I'd planned?
So quiet, so dead

Another red wine soothes the heart
A lonely party
Just temporary relief
I am doing what I want
Or am I?
Question or belief
I smile and say goodbye

Some people make you open your eyes
Others make them want to close
But people make you a person
Without them you are lost
Alone
Play a game, but at what cost?
Eyes sink dry as heated bone

The fire is alive
Flickering, jumping, sparking
Giving warm comfort
Good thoughts
Thoughts of home
In clouds I roam
Honesty or just lost thoughts?

Worms

The worms beating the mind,
Emptiness compared with truth.
To dabble in shades of confusion,
Only strengthens resolve to lose.

Bones ache with subtle despair,
Craving the wind, the tide.
Likened to disease, the past envelopes,
Devouring logic, thickening the frost.

The rock screams of life past,
With changes etched by unseen forces.
Elements of living surrounds,
Breaking bonds and myth.

A life force becoming curdled,
With each bite the worms sink deeper
To ensure you bleed without the knowing
In lies—the secret to their seduction.

The Politics Of Clown Phobia

Pied pipers for the Devil's pleasure,
Conduits for evil and dread.
The concubines of Hades,
Loyal to the abyss of darkness;
The destroyers of souls and
The keepers of torment and shame.

Platitudes woven into smiles —
Deformed, twisted, sinister smiles
Creased with time and hate.
Seething with vengeance and spiteful wrath,
Hearts blackened by a disgusted, lost past;
Souls tortured by a consuming present.

Faces hidden, disguised through fear —
Fear of being discovered, exposed.
Fear breeding anger - breeding resentment;
Meanwhile the veil, the mask,
False perception, distorted reality —
Crooked faces with crooked thoughts.

Distracting the naive with appealing talent,
Juggling truly innocent minds.
Glorifying the dim-witted,
Praising the clumsy and inept
Whilst raping the thoughts of the unwary
And sucking the life from childish purity.

Withered, empty, hungry souls
Thirsting for attention, centre stage.
Scrounging for each morsel, every scrap
Of praise from those hypnotically deluded.
Neither shame nor regret, just evil—
The blackest of evils whose victim is innocence.

The bogeymen of daytime dreams,
Wielding tools of cheap plastic savagery—
Drained of dignity, void of goodness.
They dance in the spotlight
Whilst lurking in the shadows
Watching, waiting, ready to strike.

So the next time you look toward a clown,
The next time you see a painted face ask
What hides behind those eyes, those lies?
What demented perversions consume that mind?
Have I seen the shroud of deceit lifted?
Or is it just clown phobia?

I believe –

The courage to face ourselves is
the truest test of character.

Disease

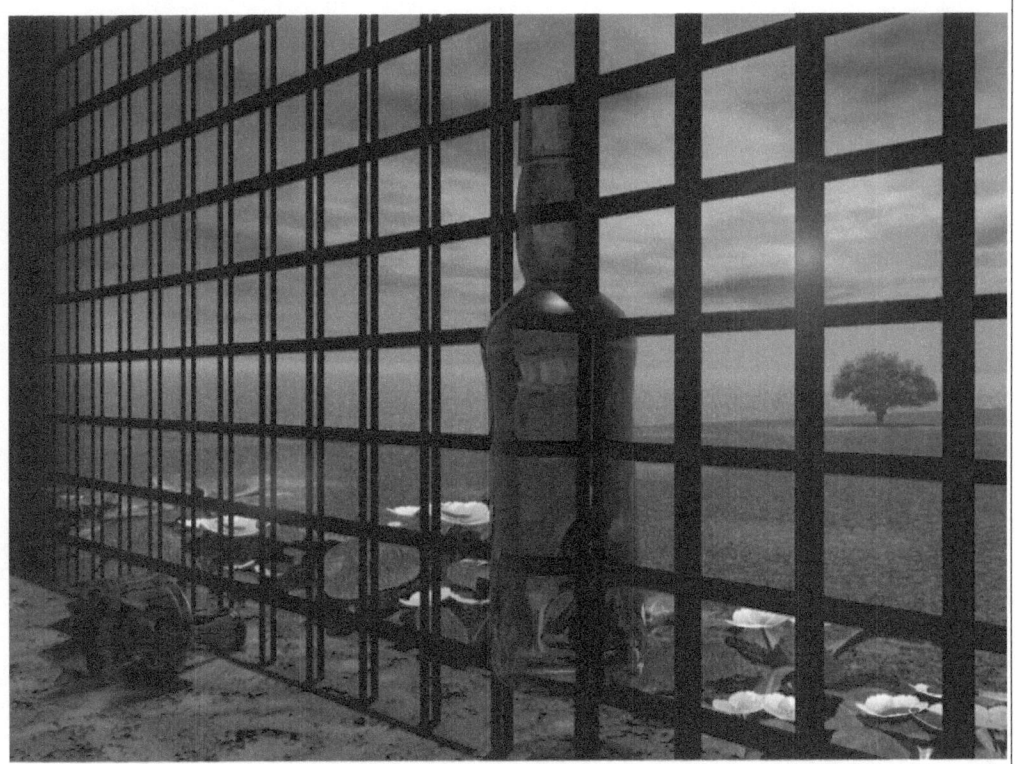

I believe –

Balance in all things maintains a soul at peace.

One Sip

The desire absolute
While denial resolute.
The conflict, sometimes rage—
Each day a warring stage.

Past shame a guiding shield,
Remembrance won't let me yield.
Destruction just one act,
A simple promise to retract.

To drop the guard and slip
Is more than just one sip;
It is to see the past replayed
And relive the wrongs I've waged.

To drink my last free breath
Is to accept defeat and death;
It is again to start my slide
Without love or hope or pride.

But for now the moment's clear
While the battle rages near.
This moment's race I've run
But I can never think I've won.

Betrayal

To my friend who died so violent a death,
My mind has killed you a thousand fold
With daggers, slowly, deliberately and desperately.
With absolute pleasure, fulfilment and gratification
I have stabbed, cut and destroyed.
I have driven you from my heart and from my mind,
Crushing as I did all memory, all reference
To that which once was
A false and misguided love.

Your betrayal has bred hatred, loathing and disgust;
Placed shadows where once there were none.
You entertained lust whilst dancing with treachery,
Sparing no thought to loyalty, to blood, to honour.
These seeds you have sown, this bed you have made—
The tangled web of your deceit shall forever be your mask.
You disposed of our friendship, our history, our future
In a moment so selfishly insignificant and brief.
And for what? Self-esteem, jealousy, ego?

Like a thief in the night, you stole, you conquered.
Your weakness, your cowardice shining like a beacon,
You spat upon righteousness, treated truth with contempt.
Trust, certainty—crushed, shattered and torn;
Dependence, reliance— scattered like dust.
Expectations of a future where our children played,
Reliance on a bond which embraced faith and hope
Gone, dissolved, devoured—for what?
Vanity, insecurity, gratification?

Should I be generous in forgiveness?
Compassionate in my moments of sadness and grief?
Should I empathise with you in your journey toward truth?
No, I think not. Just die. Just suffer.
Just rot in the putrid cesspool you think of as life, as living.
Although dead to me, I still wish to you a fate worse than finality.
May your punishment be conscience, principle,
Realisation and the understanding of your moral sin.
Carry to your grave an enormous sense of loss and guilt.
May you end your days lonely and bitter—
A victim of consequence.

To my friend who died so violent a death,
My mind has killed you a thousandfold.
Is this my pain that accompanies loss?
So unbearable I stoop to your level—
Vengeful, spiteful and rancorous.
The loss of innocence, the demise of naivety—
Should I mourn these things or learn and discover?
Should I return in kind your brutality, your cruelty?
While living as the revulsion consumes ...

Sorry—no.
You are no more and I remain free!

Regret

So sad the face of a regretful man—
Cold eyes, void of life's spark;
Dulled by pain, anger and loss.
A face revealing the approach of a harsh and bitter end
To what should have been a shining existence and conclusion.

To have grown old chasing youth,
Realising too late that a lifetime has passed.
And to have spent today pursuing distant tomorrows
Only to discover you can't catch the horizon.
Waste and emptiness, so sad the cost.

So sad the tears of a single lost soul,
The cry of lonely realisation.
Mourning missed chances and opportunities
To finally comprehend the gift and brevity of mortality,
Yet to do so only when inevitable Eternity approaches.

Then to plead for Destiny to give up one last breath
In the hope that redemption and forgiveness may be found.
Still ignorant, pathetically lost—
Unaware life's clock may never be rewound.
So fruitless that pursuit, so sad the final light.

So sad the shattered heart of a broken man
Once filled with strength, resolve and love.
Now glazed only in failure and defeat;
Consumed with scorn, bitterness, apathy—
Conquered by the nature of life.

Unable, unwilling or incapable
Of stemming the blackest of tides.
Casting aside the pride, the dignity, the honour
That was once youthfully natural,
So sad this soul's demise.

So sad the man without a dream.
Determination crushed, ambition quiet;
Desire quelled, passion and excitement subdued
By misfortune, by the reality of living,
By the strain of adversity and challenge.

So as dreams melt away and desires fade,
Life's light flickers and begins transforming
Into the selfish acts of submission and acceptance.
And with it the onset of decay, in both mind and body,
So sad the death of a spirit.

So sad the truth of regret,
Each single drop of water seemingly benign
Then years producing rivers, producing oceans
Drowning all conscious will, the instinct to survive
Flooding the very being with surrender.

Eventually, inevitably, consuming hope and faith,
Erasing every fibre, the very essence of living.
Eroding all that which makes man whole.
And death slowly, ever so slowly, stalks—
So sad that end.

I believe –

**It is better to embrace the inevitable
than resist it.**

Time

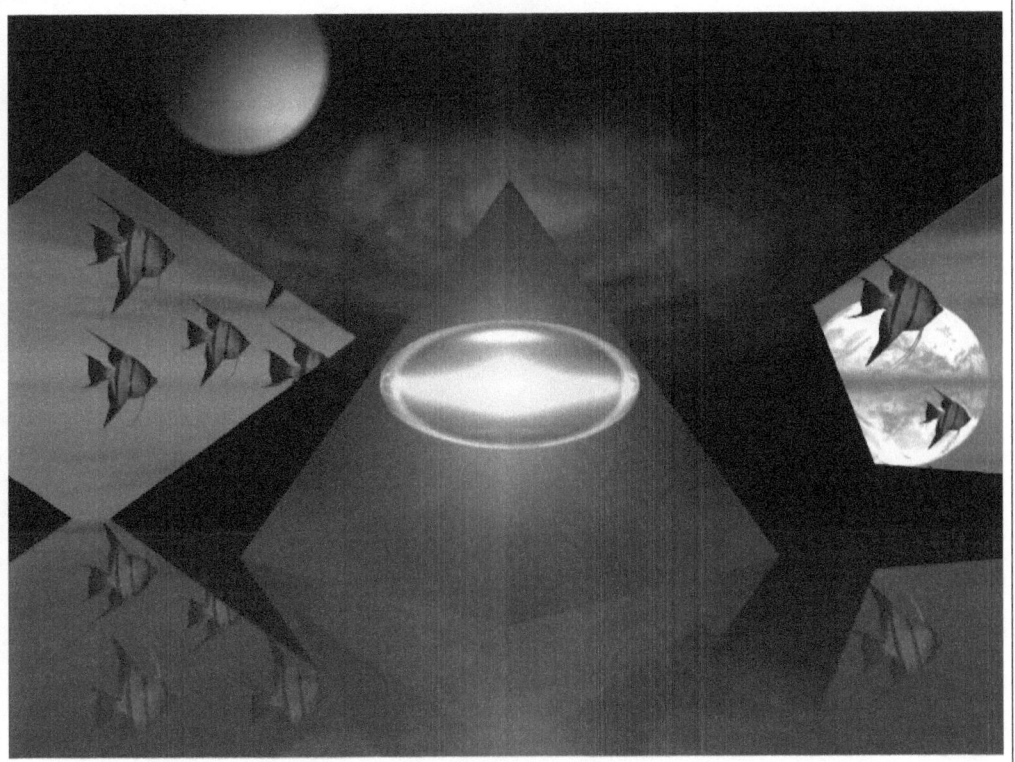

I believe –

We each have something beautiful to offer.

Age

Unseen shore, haunt me not,
Cascading waters rise.
Thoughts within clouds of mist
It's me they despise.
Changeling.

Sleep with the past, regret not deeds done,
The crooked smile persists.
Serpents whisper
Know right from wrong
An apple for the preacher.

All tinsel—glittering gold and almost bold
Your words.
Am I to swallow that which is fed?
Who is my teacher?
Them?

I am judged by imperfection, can't you see?
Minorities aren't wrong,
What is it that I should be
Conformist or lackey?
Candy-cotton clouds I miss.

To see the stars from a child's eye,
A sweetness forever gone.
My world shrinks,
Age-encircled in time,
Innocence lost.

I see a light, tread the same path.
Who is right?
Do you look at me and laugh?
Spit into the night?
Dream your dreams in a cage.

Raindrops, heaven and tears,
Golden perfection.
Cast aside misbegotten fears,
It's your own path—
Enjoy the age.

Time

My vision clouded, my judgement flawed.
Priorities inconsistent with my true heart,
A life in the process of waste.
So is the pursuit of misguided feelings and insecurities.

Lost for so long in a void surrounded by answers,
Blind to the truth and unable to escape.
So many moments swept away now drifting in darkness,
Never to be regained, relived or revisited —
Ignorance.

A sadness grips my heart; to imagine, to regret,
To know that I have been trapped
In a paradigm of my own making.
To have wrongfully believed that the most precious gift,
A gift so wondrous that it shielded my mind from all else,
Was the most precious gift of all —
My family, my children, my love for you.

I have sinned in failing to recognise that another gift exists;
One unequalled, yet taken for granted;
A bond, common to all things —
Time.

To have squandered moments chasing unseen ghosts
And to have dwelled on the past rather than accepting the present.
To have entertained petty jealousies,
Allowed hate to enter my heart;
And to have been small and weak.

When moments of strength were needed
I have preached the view of a half-full glass
Whilst embracing a half-empty philosophy.
These things I have done without seeing the truth,
Without accepting a simple reality—
The Moment.

Precious drops of time I shall spill no more
As I become consumed with all that has been granted me—
Family: encompassing love, hope and future.
All the devils and demons have been silenced.

An ignorant man's petty pursuits I have laid to rest
As my heart, my mind, my soul and my being begin to live,
Devoting each breath, each pleasure and moment
To all facets of the love and the life we share—
Contentment.

Time, the most precious of gifts is an empty vessel without love;
A tree without fruit when spent looking back upon a path walked.
You have given me the vision to see what needed to be seen,
Opened my eyes and my heart to a blossoming flower—
Our lives, our love, our children, our future.

A flower whose life is limited to just a short span
And one that needs to be nurtured,
To be loved and encouraged to grow.
And so, my solemn oath to you
Is but one word, one thought—
Commitment.

Music

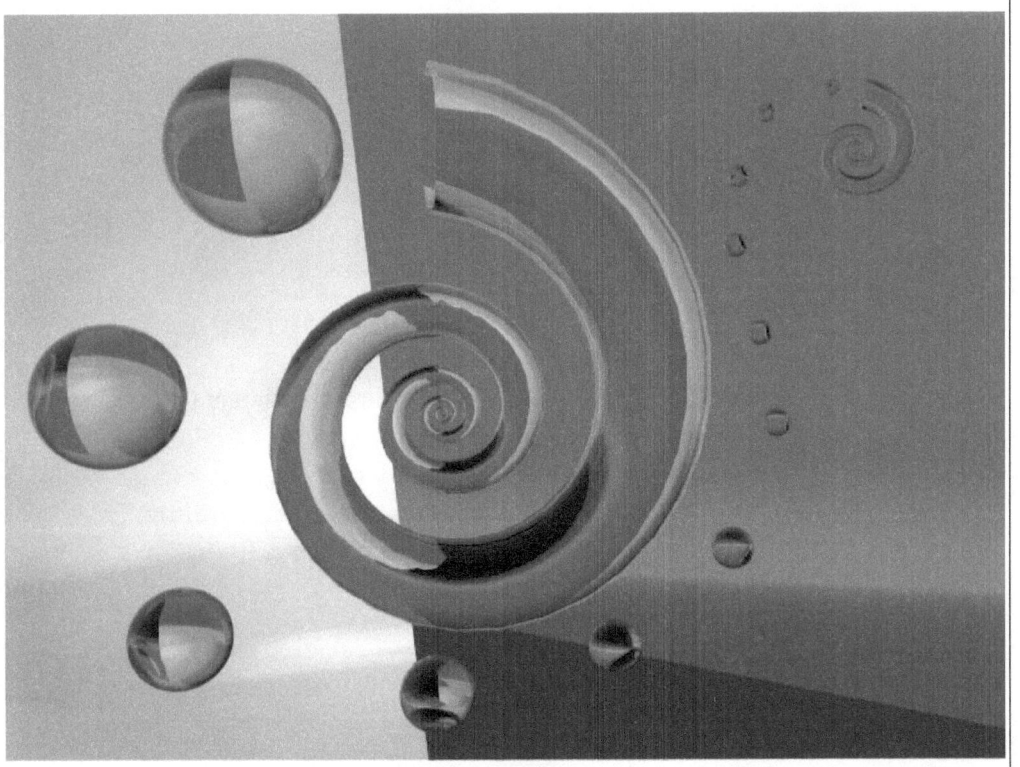

I BELIEVE

A spirit soaring on an air of faith
Does not hear the crows below bellowing defeat,
Or view the world with apathetic eyes.
A spirit soaring shares the joy of being,
With those whose hearts and minds are open and willing
To embrace all the wonders which fulfil our lives.

My Passions

Fast and furious, life lived for the moment.
Chasing excitement, adrenalin and lust—
One goal, one dream, one ambition.
Physical desire, cravings of the flesh;
Seemingly content in my pursuits
Yet harbouring desires for more.
Not knowing how to fill that unseen void,
Not knowing where or who to turn to for answers;
A piece missing from my life's jigsaw.
In truth, simply lost.

You entered my life, bringing with you hope,
Giving substance to a future whilst opening my heart.
I could for the first time see the pain, feel the loss,
Relate to the emptiness and identify the cause—
Loneliness, longing, the desire to be loved.
The passions I embraced, cultured and shared
Became embedded and entangled within our lives.
Yet the nature of those feelings would slowly erode our love,
Melting away mutual trust and the common direction we sought,
Revealing cracks in what I thought to be solid.

Familiarity, the mother of contempt,
Raising her head to deliver blows of malcontent;
Wrenching me back to a forgotten path of hidden memories,
Shattering what had been built and driving us apart.
Whilst desperately clinging to all that I love and hold dear,
Again it was you who cleared my mind and opened my eyes
By providing the reason and the will for change.
You gave me the strength to confront the blackness, deny the evil;
To accept my weaknesses and failings, understand consequences—
To see that life can and must go forward.

Like a phoenix rising, I can push aside the ashes,
Marvel with such clarity at a truth that has always been before me;
Grasp the beauty that I never understood was within my reach,
Appreciate the love and all the blessings that I have been granted.
The passions I once embraced will always be a part of me;
They shaped me and have proved to be my destiny
Yet they now pale by comparison to what lies within my heart.
A passion far greater, far more satisfying and fulfilling
Than all that has preceded it; a passion like no other—
My passion for a life in love with you and our children.

My Love

I have lived, loved and died a thousand times
In a search, a desire, a quest for love.
Bending in the wind, changing with the tide,
Forever mindful that destiny would play it's hand
And fate would eventually bring me all I sought—You!

In a field of flowers you stand alone—
Uniquely beautiful, captivating and alluring.
All things wondrous pale by comparison,
Wilting in your presence, failing to flourish.
For your heart is pure and your beauty unmatched.

In a night of stars you shine the brightest,
Illuminating all that you touch with the light of your love,
Blazing a trail for my direction, goals and dreams.
When apart, all else dulls and life loses its lustre
And returns only as I immerse myself in the glow of your soul.

In an ocean of dreams you are the clearest—
Your depth of hope, divine inspiration, unimaginable.
You embody the very essence of the future.
Giving vision and clarity where at times none exists,
You quell sinking loneliness whether together or apart.

In a lifetime of sunsets you are the most beautiful.
Captivating, consuming, inspiring and charming,
You set alight all my horizons, all my dreams,
Warming every facet of my soul, burning magnificently—
Keeping the fire of passion alive within me

In a world of flaws you are my perfection.
Tender, caring, loving and compassionate,
You give strength to my weakness, reason to love,
Meaning to passion and breath to life.
You are my sanity in a world of pain and madness.

To love you more than life is to know these things.
It is to believe and live within the wonders you provide.
This journey, my quest, has finally ended;
For no one else could fulfil or encapsulate my heart's desires—
You are my soul mate, my friend, my life.

Scottish Rose

Pictish kingdom, with roots from afar,
From the valley of the Euphrates your peoples came.
Burdened with trials, torments and unchartered lands,
Yet still they came—to tame, to grow, to embrace a future.
With ambitions, aspirations and dreams the driving force,
Into a world unknown they drifted, loved and died.
It was to be their Eden, their paradise.
And to this land they would bestow the name, Alba.

To Dalriata, Ireland, six brothers set to make their mark,
Heralding from Scota, a most beautiful pharaoh's daughter.
Of Erc, their blood and to all they would be known as Scots:
Striving, proud, and determined, with destiny held in their palms.
With Pictish eyes, desires and hopes,
They too saw Alba and embraced her as their own.
Living, loving, becoming as one with her peoples and lands,
The seeds of a new race, a new beginning were planted.

Norman conquest, Saxon reign, Viking plunder and pillage.
It was the way as centuries passed, drifting like black mist
Into the annuls of time—romance, revenge and treacheries.
Colourful threads of folklore, like fabric woven into history,
Creating legends and myths, stories and memories.
The Bruce, Roy Mac Greggor, Iona Abbey and Edinburgh castle,
Each pivotal in history, a future,
Shaping a nation, giving rise to the true Scottish spirit.

As the winds of time blew, our fate was foretold,
Destiny and its chain would draw us together.
From an ocean of tears, blood and loving hearts,
Our love would emerge, grow and prevail against the odds—
A perfection born, nurtured and caressed under distant stars,
Stars that would blaze a trail across the heavens, the past
Guiding Cupid's arrow through the ages to my heart,
To you—my one and only true love.

"Beauty, fair enough to make the world dote",
For within your heart burns the passionate fire of Scotland,
A flame which consumes my every desire, my every breath.
Your eyes hold the sparkle of a thousand Celtic nights,
Reflecting a soul that embodies all that is truly Scottish—
Strength, compassion, hope and tenderness.
A soul that I love with all my being, all my worth,
You are my destiny, my life, my bonnie lass—
You are my "Scottish Rose".

Mind's Eye

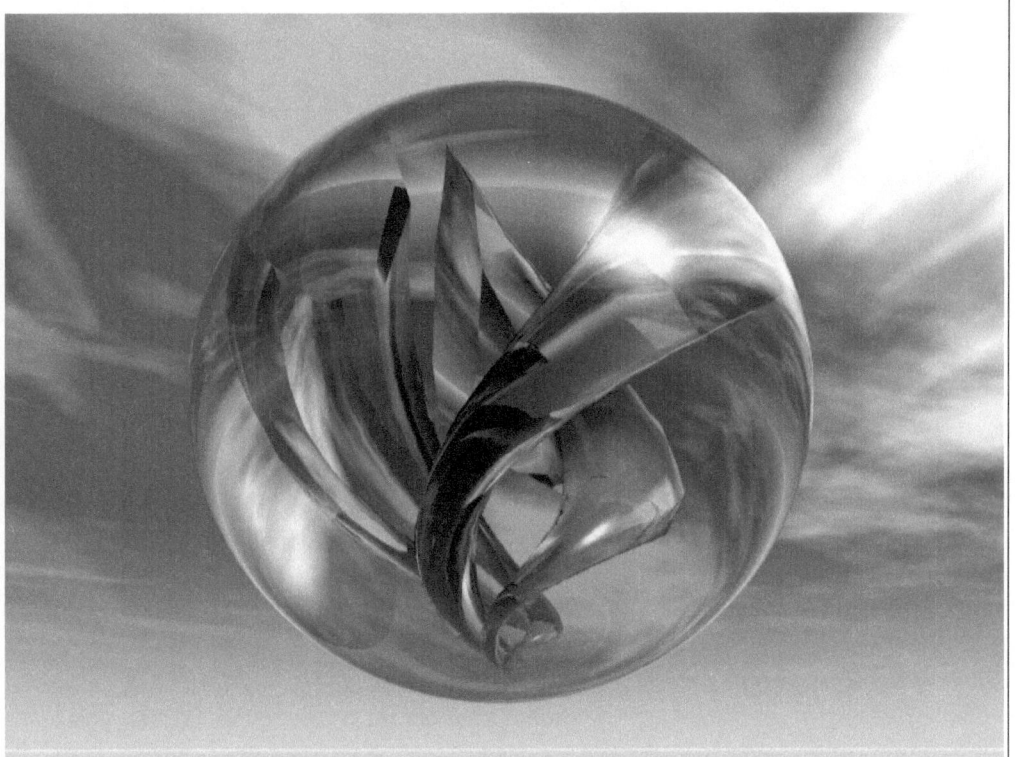

I believe –

The mind inhibits the mind's potential.

Faded Rose

Faded rose upon the morning mist,
Faded rose by dew drops kissed.
White horses trot through lush meadows green,
Lightning strikes within her dream.

Bagpipes play, a ghostly mist moves in,
Her youth is lost she knows no sin.
Her pretty smile lights the probing night
To dance with clouds, it must be right.

The air is brisk, the grass crisp and clean;
A fading moon with silver sheen
She feels alone, yet can't be sad.
A lifetime past that's not been bad.

Faded rose trapped by the years,
Faded rose with lonely tears.
She walks barefoot through memory lane,
Her aging face shows lines of pain.

A star shoots over, to earth it's bound,
In a shining instant her wish is found.
The horses prance to amazing grace—
A vision of love, she'll find her race.

A single tear trickles down her cheek,
From life's cauldron, one more sip she'll seek.
She sees the angels taking flight,
The heavens will open when the time is right.

Faded rose you'll soon be free,
Faded rose in the heavens you'll be.
Her soul's windows gently close,
Once again she's a full-bloom rose.

She sees the horses now have wings,
To the bagpipe music her angel sings.
She gently fades as her soul moves on,
Worldly pains, at last, long gone.

The Old Man's Stare

Jet black pin hole wrapped in time
Greying at the edge dulled by a past
Unknown, unseen, unspoken.
And yet blatantly, strikingly obvious,
The surface seemingly void of all things.
But deeper, much deeper—
Sadness, contentment, love?
A life.

Blending black hole
To a mass of blue grey.
Single lines, many lines
Stretching outward, intertwined;
Revealing what was once clear blue—
Young blue, innocence, naivety, youth
Long gone with age with time,
With life.

Both set in a sea of white
Again dulled by the surrounds
Bleached with blood.
Decades of blood, years of tears
Both joyous and grieving,
Hateful and forgiving,
The windows to his soul—
To his life.

Deep lines sculpted by experience
With stone like permanence
Caress the eyes, cradle them;
Somehow sharing one path
Whilst trying to protect a past.
The battle scars, failing in their mission
To disguise the truth,
Hide a life.

What is it about that stare
That haunts me, taunts me?
To look deeper, to dive into unknown realms.
To find answers to questions
That youth has not yet let me see.
Why do I need to see that depth
To feel what lies behind that old stare?
Could this stare be me?
My destiny?
My life?

I believe –

True friendship knows no bounds.

Jade

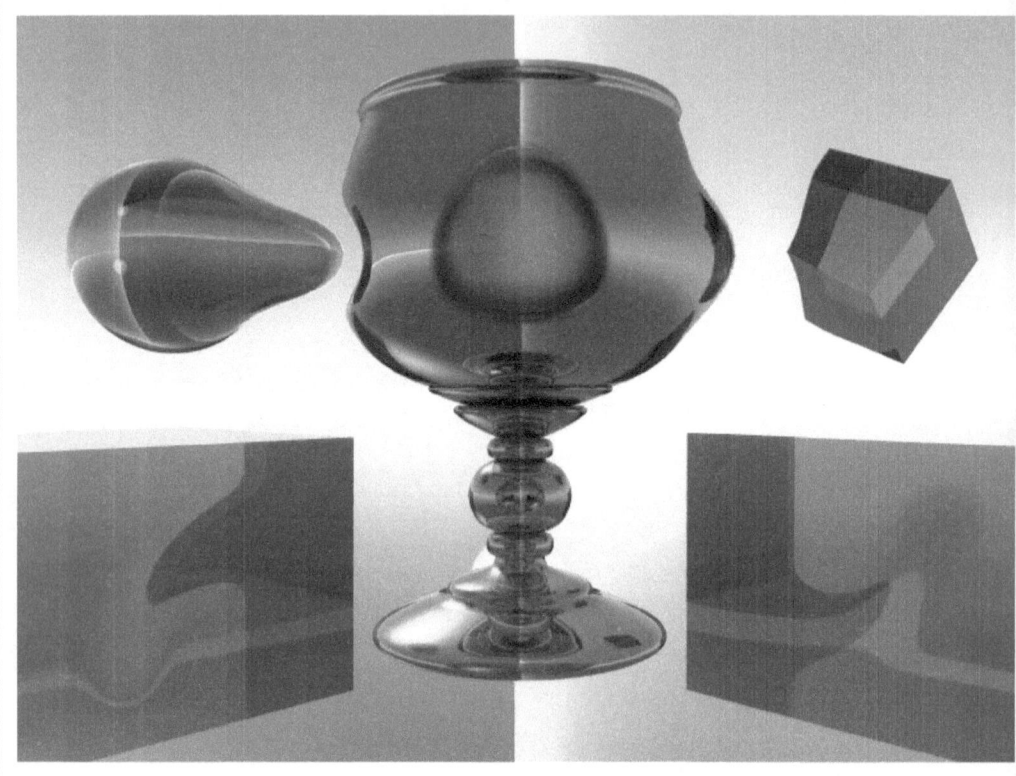

I believe –

To remain indifferent to change is to regress.

Memory Lane

I took a stroll down memory lane
With its pain, it's joy and illusion.
The girls are beautiful and alluring
While the con men smiled, hands reassuring
The show will be grand
So sensual, so seductive.

And yet as I walk the same walk,
See and smell that past,
I know that I am cast in a different time;
One of true beauty, one of tangible seduction—
My life now.

I took a stroll down memory lane;
For a brief moment lived again
A distant past so near—
Adventures, conquests.
I tasted glory, primal lust.

For a moment I was thrust into a bygone era
Where work was only
A means to an end?
And Kings Cross my hunting ground.
Again I return to my life now.

I took a stroll down memory lane.
Honestly, what can I say?
A life once lived, once loved—it was all a part of me.
That time has long since gone,
And for all the drinking, parties and loving,
I love my life and have moved on.

So Warm

A savageness swirls within the storm,
The cruelty abates when the atmosphere's warm.
So why the game when the result is blood?
Is this the way of modem love?

So much pressure, so is our way.
Plead, don't leave, it is to fight another day.
It is only the mind that weathers that storm—
So warm, so warm.

A bitter taste has crossed my lips,
The passing of lovers on distant ships.
The smiles of old memories and laughing lies
Reach without touching warn drawn eyes

Please bring me back childlike memories sweet
Or the times where cloud monsters could be beat.
Another worm, another dawn
So warm, so warm.

Correct the anxious, ignore your calling,
Pay homage to all those angry, those still falling.
I see the crash as an evil blackness stalks.
I see it, for I lived and in blood it walks.

Ignore the strain of my maddening cry
For once I died as life passed me by.
Now my tears are for another's cold storm.
I live, so warm, so warm.

Harmony

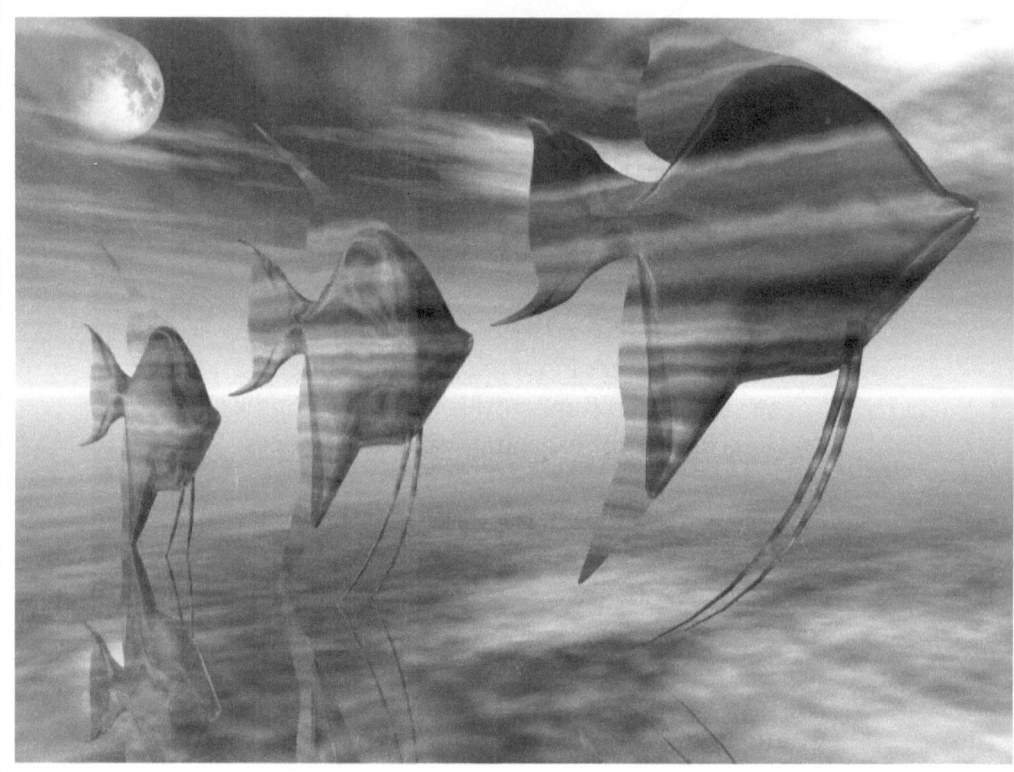

I BELIEVE

Until the hunger for spiritual advance
Is equal to the desire for technological gratification,
Humanity will remain burdened,
Like a child struggling with a responsibility
That exceeds the wisdom of his years.

Growth

Little caterpillar inching;
Growing, gaining wisdom.
Enter your chrysalis when the time is right,
Flinch only briefly to see what you left behind.
Curl and dream your future.

Little caterpillar inching;
Singing songs of freedom.
Have the wise spoken while you sleep?
Has the light entered your isolation,
Breaking free past bonds?

Little caterpillar soaring;
Your inching days are gone.
A view vastly altered,
A future filled with hope.
Will you make good use of your new wings?

Screams

Screaming when they look at me
Through eyes twisted and worn.
Soft delusions dressed scantily,
In a web of smiles and thorns.
Crooked dreams with motives poised
Amid a cloud of haze,
So subtle the thought as madness stares,
Draped in lying praise.

We wear our walls and hide all truth,
As the mind consumes the stage.
Expectations, ego and honest pain
Have given way to a flow of rage.
Mortality accepted—my father the man—
The pedestals have turned to dust.
So I paused for a moment to see the light
And discovered I had lost their trust.

So sad the screams of strangers past
Who smiled throughout those years.
They called me friend and shared my pain
Then drowned in their own fears.
So when the screams of distant dreams
Stalk and haunt the child within,
I take the man I am today
And smile an honest grin.

For without the truth and a steady path
I will wallow once again
In the stench of self-pity and loneliness
And prove I yearn the pain.

Creation

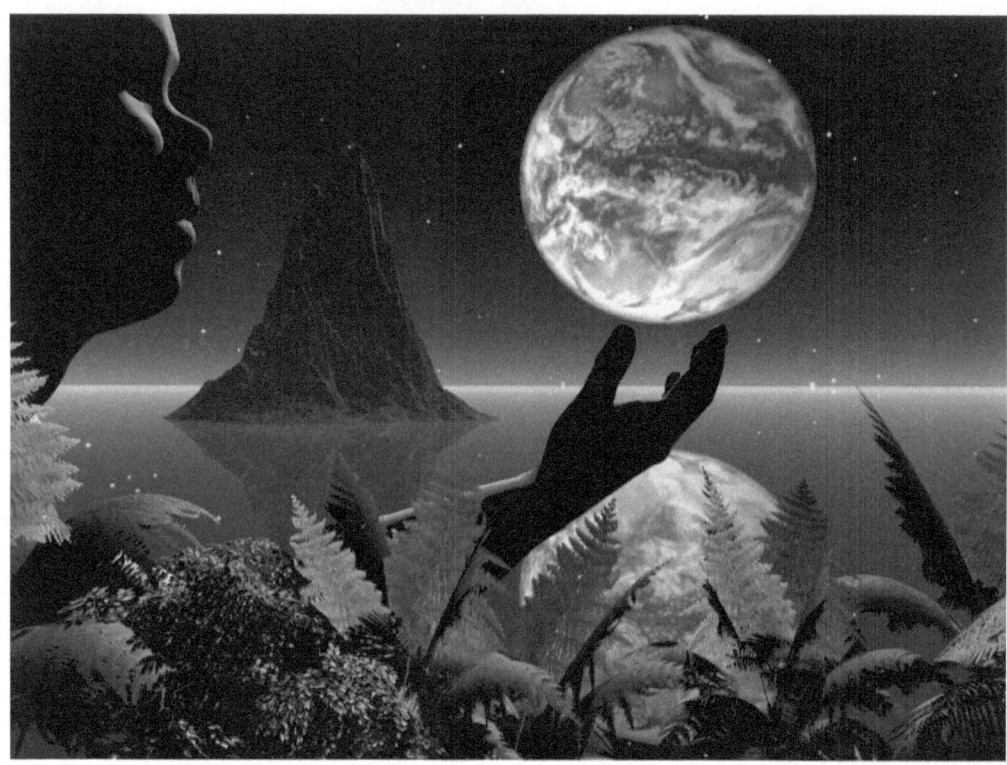

I believe –

In a Higher Power who listens to hearts,
not words.

Crushed Violet Beds

Mother Nature whistles
A song so sad, yet sweet.
For she bears no malice
In this land at heaven's feet.

Mice now on the thistles
Oblivious to the winds of time.
How lucky they must be
Not to hear the age-clock chime.

A universe inside each rain
Drop glistening within the night.
A never ending circle,
A solitary plight.

Eroding waters crash
On every lonely beach;
Romantic, frantic, ceaseless—
Do we listen while they teach?

With every passing mirror
I see a brand new face.
My mind is growing stronger
While my body loses pace.

Reflections in the eyes,
Windows to the soul—
Crystals that know no lies
Keep our bodies whole.

Innocence smiles in the face of a child
For they don't yet know of pain.
A black and white world,
An honest world,
Answers simple and plain.

So why does life grip our hearts
And often tear to shreds
The very thing we love,
Care and live for
Against crushed violet beds.

Seduction

From glistening tongue,
Her music poised to do battle.
The gentle curl of the words,
Petals caressing the desire, the need.
They consume, envelop and betray
The ache, the yearning.
That which for so long lay hidden.

The universe of her gaze,
Hypnotic in contradiction.
Purity revealing cunning, revealing innocence;
So fluid her suggestion, her plea—
Milking the moment while denying choice.
Electrifying the very essence of being,
She takes me in my entirety.

Soft abyss where I would surely fall,
Sweet surrender consumed with passionate delight
Inching tenderly, tentatively
Toward unseen shores and fields of pleasure.
Physical bliss, spiritual completeness
I fall without a hint of defiance
So lovely that which envelops my all.

I believe –

**The greatest gift we can give those
who die for the sake of humanity
is remembrance.**

Waste

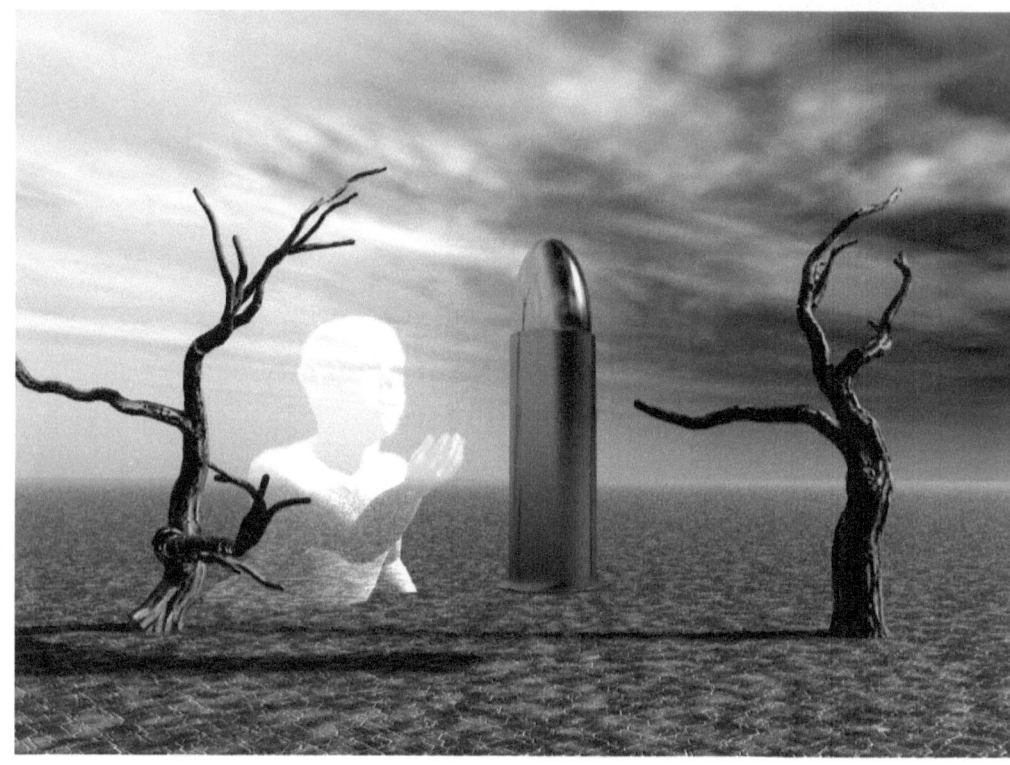

I believe –

True friendship knows no bounds.

Lights Of Dili
(*Food For Thought*)

Toward the lights of Dili, what is that you see?
Home, innocence, suffering, injustice.
Do you complain inwardly at the anguish, the pain of absence,
Or empathise with those whose indignity lies beneath shadows,
Whose blood forges a future, breathes life into a new nation?

Are you willing and able to set aside your loss, your anger?
Overcome adversity, appreciate with clarity the role you play,
Or will you close your eyes to humanity, compassion and reason
While revelling in your own self-pity and shame.
Beyond those lights, what is it that you see?

The greatest pain we endure, our ultimate sacrifice
Is not the political bunglings or the confusion of power,
Nor the uncertainty of each passing day.
It is not another night being unable to taste normality;
Nor the drudgery, monotony or routine of each wakened breath.

The deepest pain to strike our hearts is that of absence—
Absence from our children, our families, our friends.
It is being denied irreplaceable moments in time,
The closeness and passion that family brings;
The stability and cohesion that friendship nurtures.

Whist doing battle with absence, our weapons of choice—
Be they commitment or loyalty, faith or charity—
Save and separate us from the rest of society.
With a strange language and abstract perceptions of life
We transcend and conquer all barriers to ultimately soar
successfully.

It is our ability to adapt, to confront challenge with determination,
To forge ahead where others would falter.
These traits are what govern our destiny, make us unique.
This moment in time is what fate has decreed
And we will as always prevail, for it is our nature.

So if doubt, loneliness and anger consume,
Remember what it is that we take for granted—
Freedom, democracy, a right to choice and speech.
Breathe a sigh of relief as you contemplate life,
The predicaments of others and the luxury of your birthright.

Appreciate that your sacrifice is merely inconvenience
When compared to the sacrifice of others less fortunate.
Stand proud knowing you served righteousness, the good of man,
Setting aside your needs to embrace and to give selflessly
To those whose only world is
One of servitude, aggression and sadness.
And next time you are staring toward that far away isle, ask
What is it that I see, in those far-off Dili lights?

Listening

Listening to the beat of nations
Whilst contemplating my own rhythmic solitude.
Destiny, heaven or my own longing for a spiritual equilibrium
For peace, contentment or joy.
Simply dull.

Listening to the cry of innocence
Entangled within policy, bureaucracy, greed.
Witnessing the sad demise of nature—pure beauty
Riddled with the bullets of betrayal, sacrifice and confusion.
Simply madness.

Listening to storms within, through ears of experience.
Seeing nothing but grey—no light, no end, no freedom.
And yet hope remains, hope thrives.
If through nothing else necessity brings forth it's breath.
Simply life.

Listening to hypocrisy, democracy, our will, our might.
Preaching right through contrary wrongs
So subtle the method, so insane the ask.
Acceptable addiction, choice in religion, don't drop that flag.
Simply survival.

Listening to the beat of nations:
Developed, developing, all remain children new to a universe.
Will we ultimately join hands, share bread and joy?
Can I live that vision, hear that beat within myself and be true?
Simply Love.

I believe –

Communication is the nucleus
of every successful relationship.

Highway

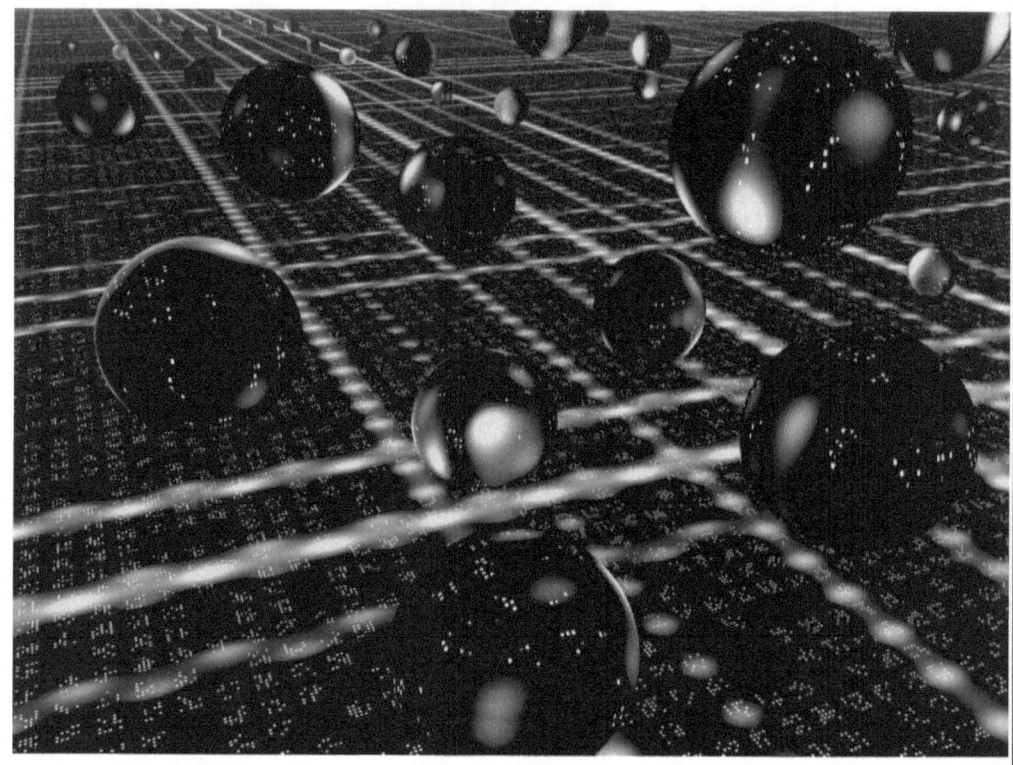

I believe –

All children deserve to smile.

Gone

An outsider looking in.
A view that can't be bested.
Strange people,
Different paths—
Each eons old, tried and tested.

No right or wrong,
Just an individual thought.
A cracked smile
Or aged frown—
But faces show the lessons taught.

Amidst a wake
Where they shall not cry
A family gathers.
Unknown relations clan as one,
What happens when we're to die.

Death Of A Boy

Coal dust, exhaustion, the violence of dreams,
Chasing a life amid the silence of screams.
Breathing in irony while exhaling death—
No choice, just chance, each day a cruel breath.

A beating, a drink, too few hours to smile,
Watching the man crawl his last lonely mile.
The irony, the twist, his life kills his soul,
Never the intention, simply the toll.

Cold war, survival, chasing technological fears,
Each a scared grin with the passing of years.
Seeds sown in silence within ice tempest rage,
The birth of a boy brings relief to the stage.

With money in mind and power feeding the force,
We set mankind on a dangerous course.
Between mines and wars and hard rolling years
We forgot to comfort our boy's lonely tears.

The bonds began breaking, initiation was lost,
And the boy was left needing while we counted the cost.
With each inch of progress man widened the gap,
The inheritance left: a boy's lonely trap.

Man's pride his champion, the yoke on his heart,
The fist on his soul with nothing to chart.
Loneliness his companion, tears dried and dead.
A single lost boy with no footsteps to tread.

A salute to progress and the casualty of change,
The fittest surviving, history the cage.
A boy with his dreams, a father one day
Who learned all his lessons while Dad was away.

And so began the cycle, a boy and his mask
Living with walls and one lonely task
To pass on the lessons he never did learn,
To teach those wanting while he continues to yearn.

So with each fallen father, a boy loses his way
And the next generation has nothing to say.
Explain the perversion, understand the greed,
The answer is plain—a father is what a boy needs.

Little White Mice Lost

Nervous people, skitting, skanting;
Little white mice lost.
Lost within the maze of life
Not knowing which way to turn.
Yearning, burning passions,
Urges, dreams,
Unbridled emotions in endless streams—
Live little white mice lost.

Each with their own direction,
Cause, belief or creed;
Each living life
Growing, loving,
Sowing one's own small seed.
Into the winds of time, each will be tossed
Like misbegotten dreams,
For we are a world of growing children—
Little white mice lost

I believe –

Alcoholism is an explanation not an excuse.

Escape

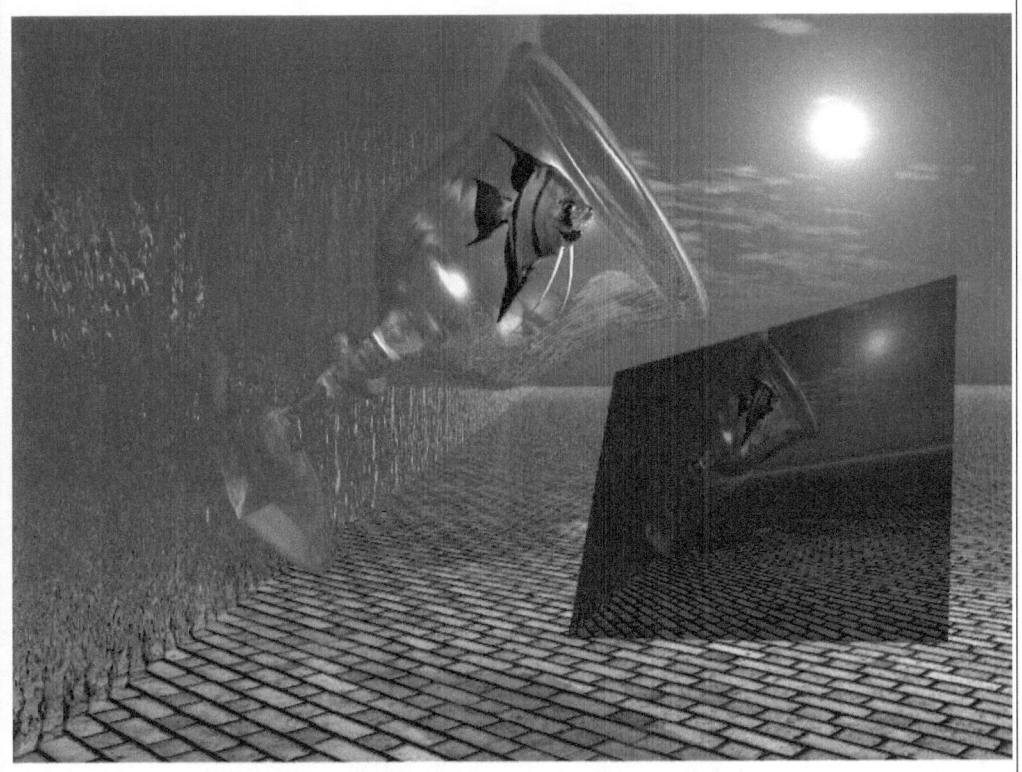

I believe –

Education is a solution, whereas prohibition is not.

Life Hurts

Content in your squalor
You eke out an existence
Forever complaining,
Contemplating what might have been,
Yet secretly at ease
With your gift to inwardly laugh
At the misfortunes of others,
People in pain.
How small you are.

Your dreams and aspirations
Seek only the next day,
Your youthful vision faded—
Crushed by life,
Destroyed by others
With as much hope and love
As you now have to offer.
A travesty your sinking soul—
Aimlessly, hopelessly drifting.
How pathetic you have become.

Compassion exchanged for pity;
Love for hate; reason for vengeance;
Passion for anger.
For all the lies, deceits and lessons
Inflicted by this harsh and unforgiving world,
It is still by your own choosing, your own hand
That you remain stagnant;
Stranded, suffocated and poisoned
By the very web you spun,
Alive in body only, a spirit departing.

To continue as you are is to regress,
To die a slow, empty death.
To pass from this world without a whimper,
Without a shout or cry for help
Is an abomination, a crime against humanity,
An insult to all those who continue to strive,
To struggle, to climb from pits of despair.
Your weakness, your apathy, your contempt
Stings the eyes and blackens the hearts of those
Who try, who embrace, who feel, who are living.

What it is that you can visualise?
You will only ever travel
As far as you can see.
Accept that life has many forms, many guises
And chase all that you can be. Are destined to
Become captivated by living?
Taste it, Live it, love it, dream it.
Ignore petty and small-minded distractions and delusions.
Just say Yes! and soar.

Live The Man

Cloth lady, strut your pretentious pose,
Forget what lies beneath the rose.
Pearl white lies and plastic dreams,
Endless days of inward screams.

Shallow man, simply lost and aged
I see the pain of instincts caged.
Feign contentment while passions die,
Foundation rock that will not cry.

Superficial smiles and wounded eyes,
With each new face, humanity dies.
Tears of chalk cry wolf with ease,
Insecure the ego that dies to please.

Chase those ghosts of youthful venture,
Is this the reward for midlife pleasure?
Childlike mountains exact soft tolls
While childish actions breed stagnant souls.

The mind desperate, thirsting eternal youth,
The mirror rebukes and speaks the truth.
Don't seek spirituality in artificial light,
Grip all your dreams and hold them tight.

And next time tempted, pretentious pose,
Open your eyes to what makes the rose
Chase that moon in cotton fields of joy—
Live the man, embrace the boy.

I believe –

Karma is a part of the natural order of the Universe.

Jewel

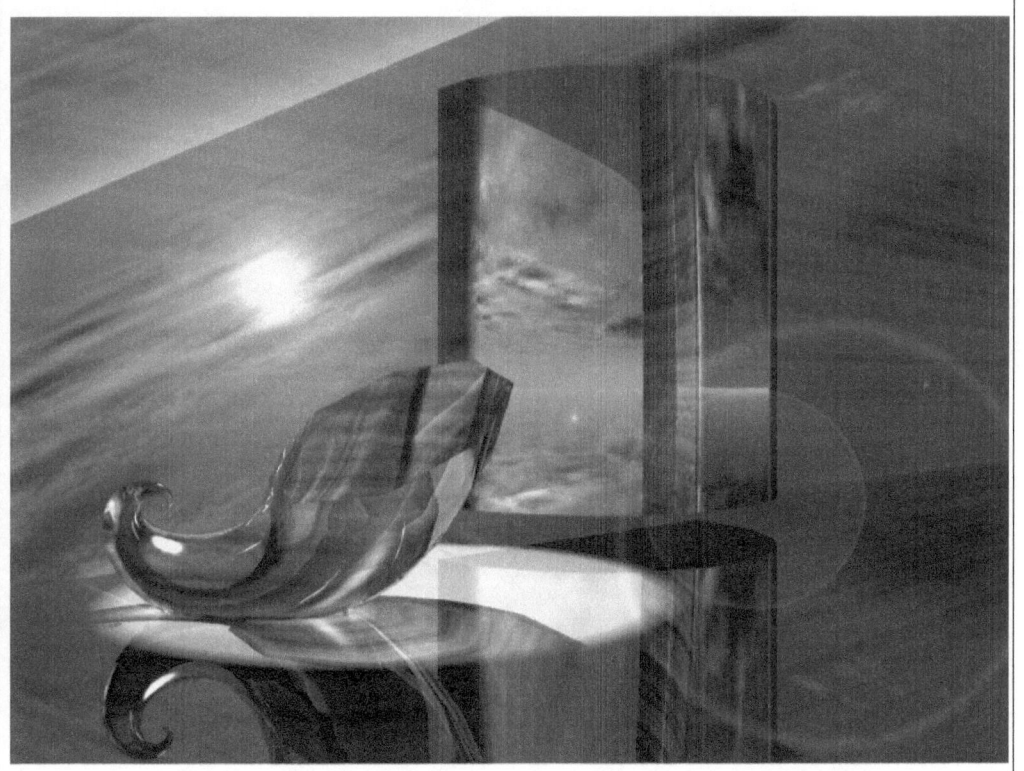

I believe –

Hatred and cruelty are taught.

Heaven's Verandah

Childhood is Heaven's Verandah,
A place where dreams are not yet tarnished by age;
A time when the world is absorbed and embraced
With unbridled imagination and pure fascination,
With a love and passion for all things new.
A gate protects this most sacred of places;
A gate which when opened may never be closed
For it leads to reality, the bittersweet path of life.
To walk this path is to put aside all those childlike things—
Naivety, innocence, virgin imagination.
And there will be no time once that journey has begun
To look back or return for those missed chances.

A rainbow refracting light,
Transforming what is unseen, taken for granted.
An array of colours, of beauty
Pure, natural, alive
Kept real and tangible by the tears of Heaven
Creating illusion, delusion.
Chase that hidden gold, that folly
In childhood, sparking imaginative journeys
To lands of giants and riches.
In adulthood, scientific curiosity
So sad the myth dying in the face of fact.

A silver streak passes across the heavens,
Highlighting a billion stars, a trillion moons,
A million dreams from a million lifetimes
Glorified, emphasised in a split second,
A most brilliant death
In that moment another dream, another wish

Is added to the splendour
For another to gaze upon, reflect
In a distant millennia, a far off time
And wish, maybe dream
What it was that passed through my mind
In that brief yet perfect moment.

A Christmas tree, solitary yet not alone in its magnificence;
Sparkling, dazzling, bringing promise and hope
Too brief a reminder of religious significance.
A symbol of unity, love, birth and freedom
Furnished with the feelings and tenderness of family,
Endeared with trinkets so cheap yet hypnotically beautiful
Paying tribute to closeness both past and present.
Childish fantasies becoming real with each flickering light,
Boxes so carefully and tenderly wrapped, lovingly placed
With crisp clean edges they await—a sea, a multitude of wishes.
Begging, beckoning, excited hands, fingers and eyes to explore,
Smiles to light a world and the warmth of any distant star.

As I allow my children to pass from one world to another,
Will I impart a vision of this world as seen through my eyes?
Love, respect, truth and beauty—
Before the gates open will their dreams be enough to fulfil them?
Enrich a life, a future, a destiny?
And as they voyage down that so mortal a path
Will they still make a wish on the death of a star
Or remember God's promise as a rainbow fades?
Will they speak fondly of sack races, days at the beach,
Candy apples, hill slides and parents who loved them?
Or smile at the possibility of Santa getting stuck in a chimney?

Will I succeed by repaying in kind all the joys that they gave me?
By furnishing their hearts with beautiful memories,
Enough to last a lifetime.
Will I succeed in preparing their way?
Equipping them for a journey where battles are won and lost,
And fought on a less forgiving playing field,
One that is incomparable to the imagination of innocence.
Will I achieve what all fathers desire;
What all fathers desperately seek for the children they love—
Strength, courage, compassion, honesty—
Before opening that gate and watching them leave
"Heaven's Verandah"?

I believe –

A soul will only find freedom through honesty.

Freedom

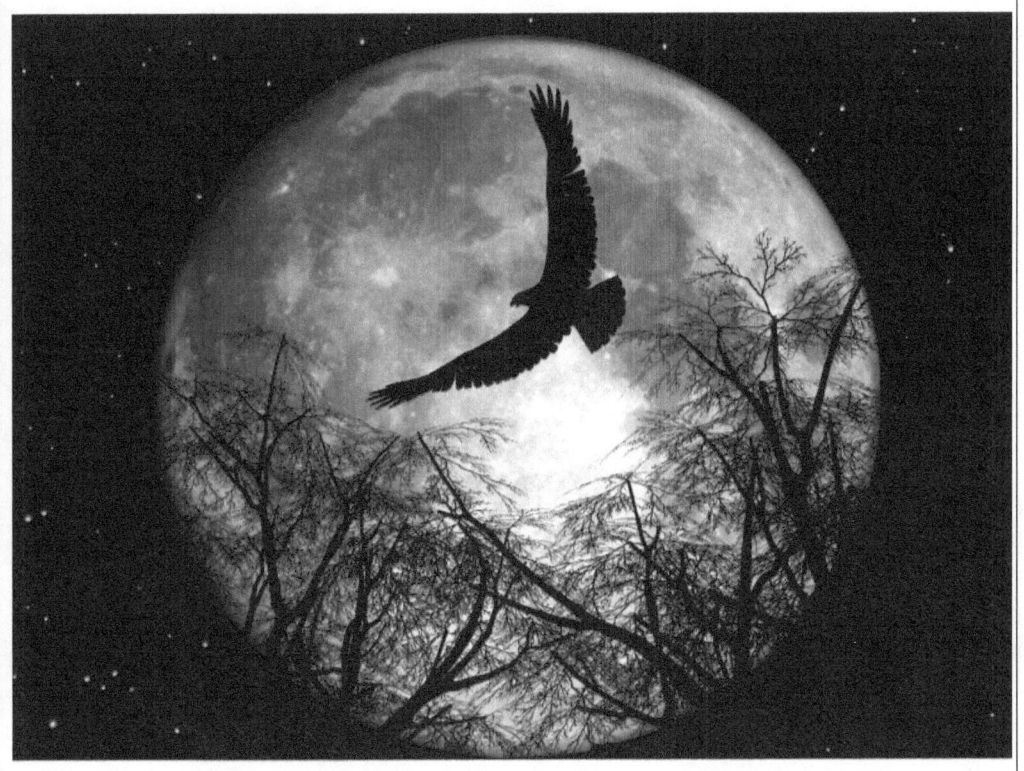

I believe –

The greatest challenge I will ever endure
Will be facing life without a crutch.

Falling In Love

Eyes glazed, my mind a thousand miles away.
The rustling of my pages, distant breeze
Wrenching me back to closer thoughts
As I scribble beneath dull light, shaded full moon.
I can't help but feel the warmth of where I have just travelled.
Inspiration strikes, gently, beautifully soothing.
A smile appears as I caress that one brief memory,
Yet all too quickly it begins to fade, so I write frantically,
Capturing on what was once blank that so perfect a moment.

A cold, rain-swept night seven short years ago.
Thunder rolled across the heavens—God's true might
Nature demonstrating her glorious power and wonder,
Filling our hearts and minds with her voice.
Lightning streaked across our own piece of this world,
Running down power lines, setting alight our street,
Splitting trees whilst cracking its way to earth.
A storm so magnificent, a prelude to love
Stimulating senses, exciting the air, the mood.

We watched while gods danced hand-in-hand
Giving life to the memories and legends of Guy Falk's
As rafters creaked and windows rattled in our old rented house.
We drifted into honest, shameless and pure conversation—
Two people, two strangers, discovering each other;
Sharing years, sharing experiences, simply enjoying
Beginning a journey without realising we had
Delved into each others lives, two souls shaking hands
Without ulterior motives, without a past, without a history.

The storm raged, gaining in strength and ferocity;
The proverbial wolf trying to smash its way into our lives.
Straining, failing to achieve anything destructive, on the contrary
Building bonds, a climate of closeness and security.
The music became louder as we duelled over trivia—
Pick the song, the year and who sang that; friendly banter,
Barriers transcended, invisible prejudices laid to one side
By the warmth of the company, the comfort of the conversation,
Content to just immerse ourselves in that time, that space.

Plunged into darkness, a night charged, electric.
The static, the energy consuming every sense, every thought.
Another blackout, intensifying the excitement, breeding romance.
Candles setting the stage, flickering, disrupting shadows;
Illuminating, arousing and engulfing the atmosphere.
At ease, we talked and walked a path toward a distant future,
Toward gifts and dreams we could never have conceived.
We cherished the night, the storm, the chemical excitement
Without fully realising Cupid's arrows were flying.

The seeds of love were planted during that distant storm,
Opening my heart and soul to a beauty which lay before me.
Could it be that destiny, fate, nature or God
Played a hand in awakening all that was dormant within me?
Preordained or coincidence,
Whatever the answer, you stoked a fire and stirred my soul,
Arousing change, exciting the passion, the breath of life.
Such a perfect moment, a uniquely beautiful aspect of our love—
Our Genesis.

Beneath the layers of life lies your true heart—
One that I have grown to know, to feel and to love;
A heart that I saw for the first time during a night of storms,
A night that was to change my life irrevocably, forever.
Within the facade of this world lives your true soul,
One that fills my being with all the joys of this earth.
A soul exposed by thunder, lightning and mother nature—
Beautiful, consuming and tantalisingly addictive.
So it is, I now understand, "Falling In Love".

I BELIEVE

A beautiful gift so freely given—
Divine intervention or the complexities of evolution,
Why not both?
Is it better to unravel the question
Or accept the wondrous mystery
And live passionately within our world?

Change

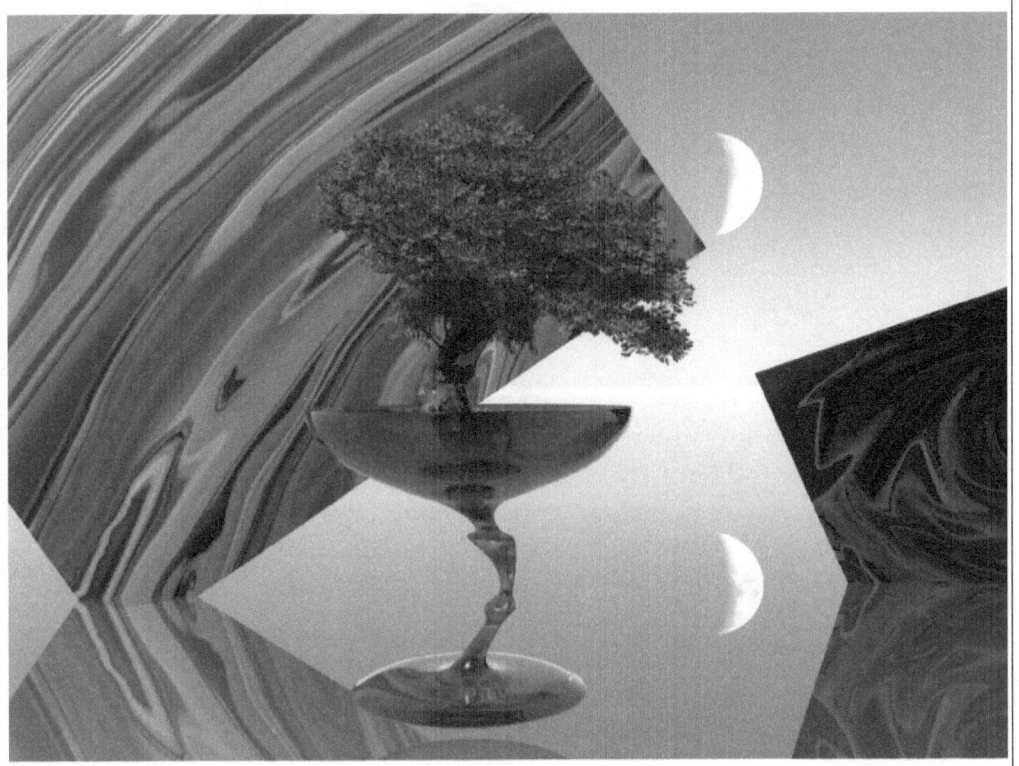

I BELIEVE

The far reaches of our minds and imagination
Cannot fathom the awesome power and expanse
Of infinite galaxies beyond our reach.
We cannot possibly be alone.

Changes

The mirror reflects
My own mind's eye.
I see while remaining blind.
Subtly, slowly nature grips
While I sleep, failing to remember
Feeling, seeing, learning
The changes.

Our eyes don't reflect, don't shine
With the same illuminated glow.
I hear, yet remain deaf.
Gradually life stalks, hunts,
Creeping incessantly silent.
I don't remember noticing, sharing
The changes.

Am I bitter, lost as I look
Off track in my train of thought.
Growing older, wiser,
Learning more whilst realising
How little I know.
Will I remember, will I see
The changes?

Have my eyes twisted the truth?
Tunnel vision, no focus—
Is my soul trapped by its own existence?
A paradigm, sin
Unwilling, not wanting to expand,
To grow, to feel, to embrace
The changes.

Wisdom brings enlightenment,
Brings age, breathes change
And yet more questions arise.
Answers elude, frustrating, nagging
Yet perfect, testing the mind,
Challenging the soul—
The changes

I adjust, open my eyes,
Bend to meet expectations.
Realisations never so near, comprehension
I ignore my stand, past views, entrenched ideas,
For it is better to accept the present,
Blend in the past, whilst embracing
Inevitable Changes.

Walls

Where are the flowers that stole my soul,
Those dreams of a world in a childlike role?
Where are the mountains that consumed my heart,
The joys of challenge, in all things a start?

When will the world see the truth of my face
Or shall the façade consume and embrace?
When will my smile be seen for the light
Distorting the dark while embracing the right?

Why are my tears hidden from that I love,
Is the shame of sharing more than enough?
Why isn't honesty my only mask?
For forgiveness or wisdom I shall not ask.

How do I live when all faith is lost?
To continue the lie is to double the cost.
How could I have danced without a true tune
And sang a dead song, giving up too soon.

Here are my words, myself, my thoughts;
My poems within, without the walls.
For a world without walls would be a thing to behold,
Flowering with love and free from the cold

I BELIEVE

Sexuality is not a matter of choice,
Bigotry and Prejudice are.
Both traits are born of fear
And deny man-kind's true destiny.

Growth

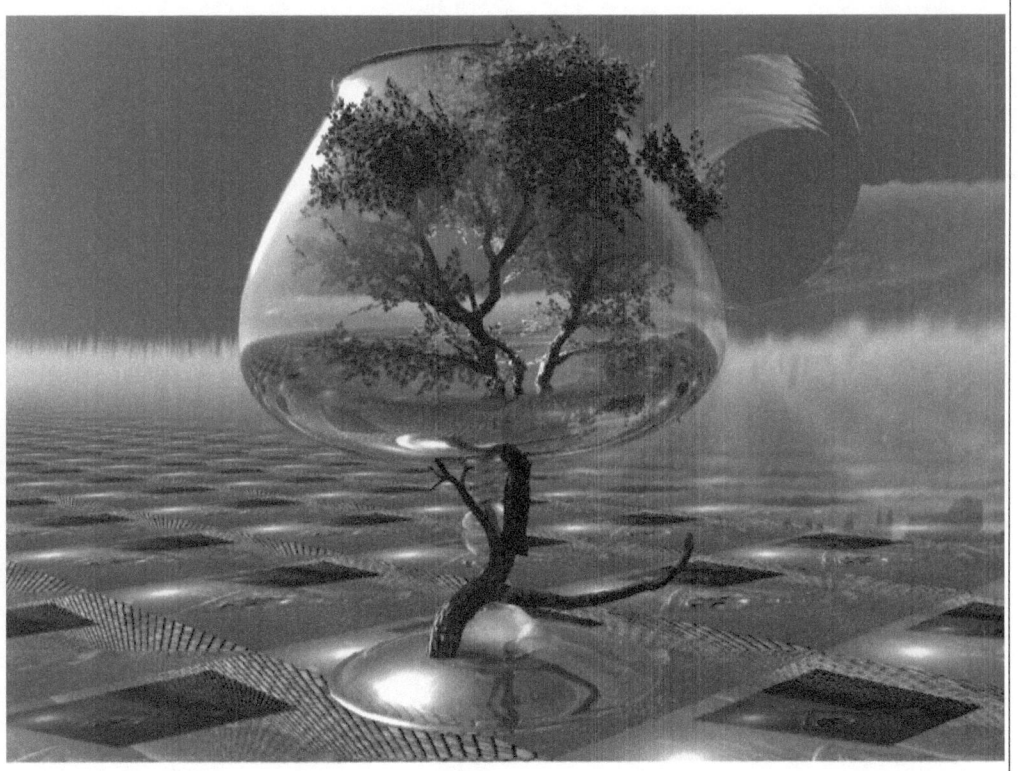

I BELIEVE

Mankind's petty differences
Will only and ultimately be laid to rest
By the might and natural order
Of the universe.

Walk In the Rain

The insanity breathes with the knowing.
Is the growing simply about acceptance
As cowards, as friends? Dine at my table.
Am I able to smile, simply able?
Shallow victories, empty crowing
And now I feel the pity showing.

The crocodile tears conveniently flow.
My weakness screams, shines like a beacon
While the hungry mouths wait to consume.
So black the hate, the pain, the weakness—
That which I keep in chains and cannot show.
So I see, in a distant heart, a distant glow.

I walk in the rain, foe and heaven's tears;
I drown the memories, live the storm
Embracing, killing all things cold.
In the joy of emptiness I revel,
Perversion dictates I embrace the fears,
In a flashing instant, my confusion clears.

With wounds once soaked in tears of salt,
I walk my path drifting, depressed, hopeful.
Is my true heart to be understood, felt?
Embraced by the hearts I love, I need,
Which key opens that which lies within the vault,
Will I finally live where honesty is not at fault?

So where is the message as I walk in the rain,
Enjoying it's touch, the feeling, the freedom.
For me it is perfection, pure, an empty contentment.
There is no message save that which lives for me.
In that storm I am free,
Embracing love, killing pain;
In that storm it is the blackness and the worms I tame.

A Social Gathering

What lies within your dormant spirit?
Suppressed, screaming, dreaming of freedom.
Bound by social expectations, contradictions,
Draped in hypocrisy and enveloping worldly ties,
What lies within your dying heart?

The smile of a child reaches deep,
Grappling with the distance of years past,
Awakening the perfection of innocence,
The beauty of naivety, exploration and discovery—
And with that breath your spirit sighs.

The music lingers sweetly, stirring your being.
Electricity shudders through your every vein
As you reflect—first kiss, first friendship, first love.
Too soon the tide shifts, so brief that moment of peace.
Again the walls of age, of pain, consume and overpower.

The wine burns your throat while distracting your view,
A bitterness not born of grape but rather familiarity;
A suffering amplified by feelings of entrapment.
Silently you endure, crying into the emptiness of time—
How long will desperation remain concealed?

The conversation drones—plastic, predictable, frustrating.
For you, the glass was always half-empty,
Your mind overflowed with doubt, insecurity and loss.
And so you became consumed by the like-minded—
Complicity your escape, your excuse and ally.

Hope stifled by surrender, faith conquered by resignation.
Have your eyes and heart finally closed for eternity,
Or have your arms and mind opened to embrace a truth?
Capture an opportunity given freely by destiny,
Will you turn your back or leap with utter abandonment?

The spark of a defining moment flickers but once.
Are you able to recognize it, embrace the power of it's worth
And ignite a passion which once flowed unbridled?
For moments past are but an illusion, distractions to tempt.
Will you choose self-pity or cast aside despair?

What lies within your dormant spirit?
The strength to pursue your passions, your loves;
The courage to sow forgiveness and tolerance
While living a decision draped in commitment?
Only you know the truth of your heart.

Coward

When illusions leave their bitter taste,
Consuming and devouring your soul
You fill your mouth with gluttonous waste?
In an attempt to again, feel whole.

Blame the world; it's your desire to bleed
You hunger the pain and excuse.
Ego and pride, your only need
While you wallow in self abuse.

Thoughts spent chasing frozen dreams
Within a tormented heart.
Faces contorted with endless screams
Each playing a deafening part.

Remember the web you chose to weave
When testing your own lies.
And remembering those you did deceive
Won't free those alibis.

Ambitions littered with pottery and pearls,
You measure in weights of gold.
Magical illusions in sweet satin swirls.
And a soul you willingly sold.

You play your part with a cowards smile
While self pity claims the stage.
You always bring the world to trial
Unable to shield the rage.

I BELIEVE

Within the pleasure of music,
The notes of friendship will always linger,
Drowning with ease completely
All but the sweetest of memories.

Haze

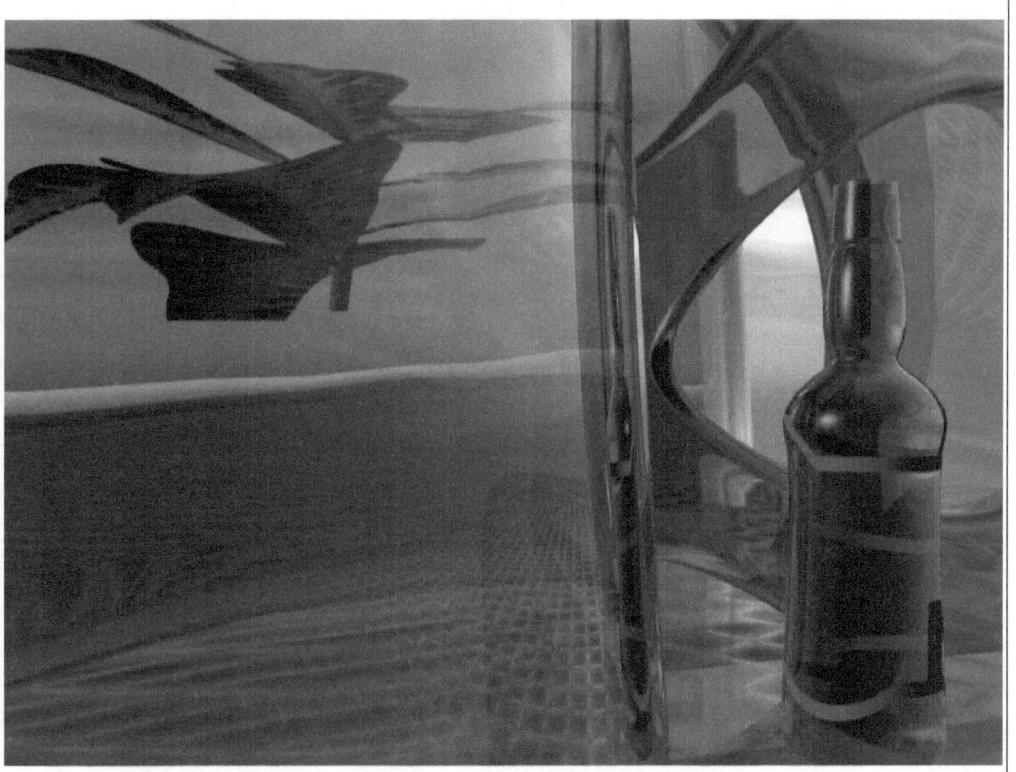

I BELIEVE

Watching the seconds sink into silence
Is to remain blind within a journey.
To listen to life's chime and rhythmic conclusion
Is to leap toward finality, deaf to the music.
To ignore the senses and breathe only time
Is to condemn all things to stone.

No Longer

I no longer feel the threat
Of my own lies,
Or know the sting
Of accusing eyes.

I no longer revel loudly
In sarcastic wit,
Or hide behind clowns
That seem to fit.

I no longer play the mouse
And chase the cheese,
Sacrifice dignity
Too willing to please.

I no longer pull the strings
That control the fear,
Or indulge an anger
When resentment is near.

I no longer live in self-pity
And blame all but me,
For without these things
I am truly free.

Drunk With A Bar Girl

I've walked in the shadows with pen and paper.
Delusions set in.
A pittance taken from cast-off receipts
She makes her living.
Dart board encircled, alcoholic mist,
The bull, the hole on green velvet table—
My life.

With wine and Brandy to Napoleon I speak
As Johnny Walker talks
A language I don't comprehend, yet answers I seek.
Flags fly but I'm not really home,
Pink walls engraved with previous visitors' stories.
She's left me.

The money's gone, as are the baubles from a seventh 21st.
What follows?
Dragons painted within fluorescent ads,
They scream
Tiger, Anchor, the haze consumes,
Feelings swirl.

Read my mind.
Sit alone, don't be blind.
Lost the edge amongst virginal gum trees.
Home or dreams,
Butterflies and dragons
She plays my lead.

Compassion, reason, inner weakness—
Money talks.
Building bricks, a child wants more.
Cash in hand, she smiles,
Dragons again stare through the dark.
Are they truly wise?

Chinese charm, the sign strains.
She stares to another.
Pretence.
You smile with me, I smile with you.
Welcome to Asia—
Money whispers!   No lies

Seduction reigns in a beautiful face;
Her touch dominates.
Poisonously sweet, talk awhile,
Never lose touch with the truth,
The love and hate, hand-in-hand down a glass aisle
I find reason where reason does not lie.

Liar

The long nights slowly turn to days,
Evil smiles in the smoky haze.
Break the bread and pass the wine,
The Devil's here and we shall dine.
Candles flicker, with a shadow cast—
Will this night be our last?

Forget-me-nots and TV's blank,
Dead tribes lost with their gods to thank.
Our heroes with medals who fought our way
Machines now punch out lives of clay.
Political riddles and a butcher's knife,
Religious traditions, a cheating wife.

Mountains capped with acid rain,
Tracks laid in death, a first-class train.
To see you with deluded eyes
And know the sin that you despise.
Calm yourself and don't get lost
Forget the pain and hidden cost.

Who really cares what you may think?
It doesn't matter, life's just a wink.
Should this be true, then what's the point?
That's right, relax, smoke your joint.
Hypocritical fire that's your forte,
Which God helps you to pray?

You write your poems for one sad song,
Do you consider you may be wrong?
You make excuses, play and drift
Then turn to others for that lift.
Have you seen the mirror and cried insane
And bled to all about your pain?

What makes you feel that you're alone,
And when did you inherit that throne?
Try to accept your living is truly done
When you choose to move on.
So as you sink and slowly tire
Think of the verse and me the liar.

I BELIEVE

When the emotional, physical, spiritual or mental cost
Exceeds the financial consideration,
A conflict will inevitably result.
Only two states exist: acceptance or denial—
Acceptance will breathe beauty into life,
Denial will suffocate and consume.

Birth

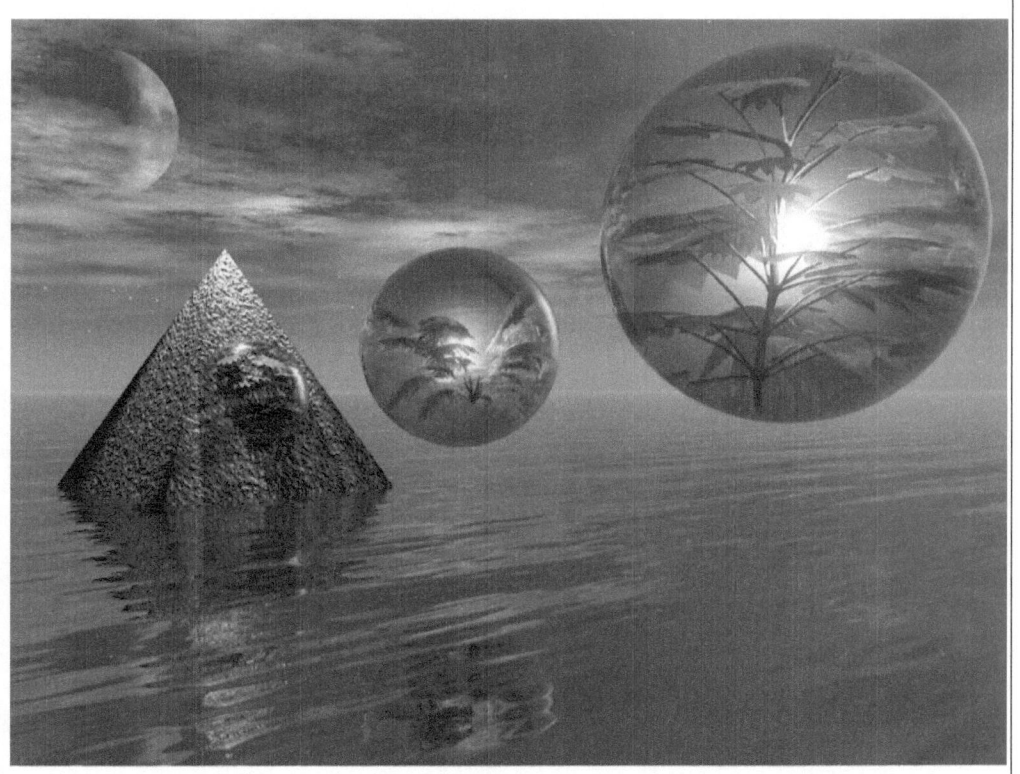

I BELIEVE

Brief moments of absolute peace
Exist only where tranquillity greets absence,
When solitary moments and clarity prevail.
To allow your soul to sigh and rest
Is to heal the wounds of another day.

Making Love

Soured by pain, jealousy, anger and hate.
A perfection shattered, purity blemished;
A field of dreams, pleasure and beauty
Now a field of battles and sorrow.

A place where magnificence shone
Now an empty victim of circumstance.
Scarred, smouldering, tense,
The vicious circles have drained life,
Transformed a sharing crowded with emotion into vacuum,
And now it begs rebirth—
Genesis.

From the ashes of a once mighty fire
Can we resurrect that erotic passion, the sexual flame?
Can we arouse desire, spontaneity, will?
And return to a time and place that we have both cherished?

Is it possible this void, this period of darkness
Is purely a prelude to greater experience?
A cocoon from which we shall both emerge
Enlightened, aware, prepared
To accept and embrace other's desires, needs and wishes
And satisfy selflessly with renewed vigour and spice.

To share once again those special moments
When the world around evaporates, dissipates into nothingness
And the only thoughts, the only feelings, the only desires
Are that of each other, pleasure given and received.

To find the place which excites
Arouses, titillates, escalates
The passion, the life and the needs we harbour
And to touch the other in a way no other has.
Pleasuring, enticing, teasing
Every fibre, every muscle and every breath of our being.

To feel the world around us come suddenly back to life
As the ecstasy, the surge of tension evaporates,
And to find ourselves more appreciative, alive and aware
Of that beautiful presence which surrounds—
Brought on by our passionate absence.
Then to lie seconds later, panting and spent,
Softly holding, stroking, feeling
The warmth, wet and soft
Of the others body, each other's exhaustion—
Cuddling, snuggling, satisfied and content.

I wish for us to paint a picture—
Your body the palette, my body the brush,
Our hearts the canvas.
Two minds joined to exploit physical and emotional desire,
To stimulate and satisfy the yearning of expression,
To climb once again to those heights of arousal, captivation;
Not for the sake of urge or indulgence
But for the gift of sharing our true selves, our true minds.
Selfishly, selflessly painting that most beautiful scene
In love, for love, making love.

My Love For You

The power of my love comes not from infatuation
    Driven by the passion of a single moment;
    Nor is it given life through shallow desire,
    Superficial dreams or simplistic instincts.

The power of my love exists not for selfishness,
    Surviving only to satisfy an insecure ego;
    Nor does it strive to ease the pain of life
    Or dull confusion and loneliness.

The power of my love grows through time and sharing.
It is the spirit of peace which resides within me.
The calm, the contentment, the warmth of being—
It is that which fills my every breath and yearning,
    My every moment.

The power of my love is you and your being.
For it is you who fills my spirit with the warmth of sunrise
And you who breathes the fire of passion into my soul.
You are my all, the sweet love which embraces my heart.

The power of my love is empty without you.
And for that which you give freely, I love you.
The power of my love is a wonderful gift
And for all the beauty which is you, I thank you.

I BELIEVE

A dream without action will remain a dream—
Until it becomes a regret.
Dreams pursued dissolve horizons and break bonds,
Setting the soul of man free.

Dawn

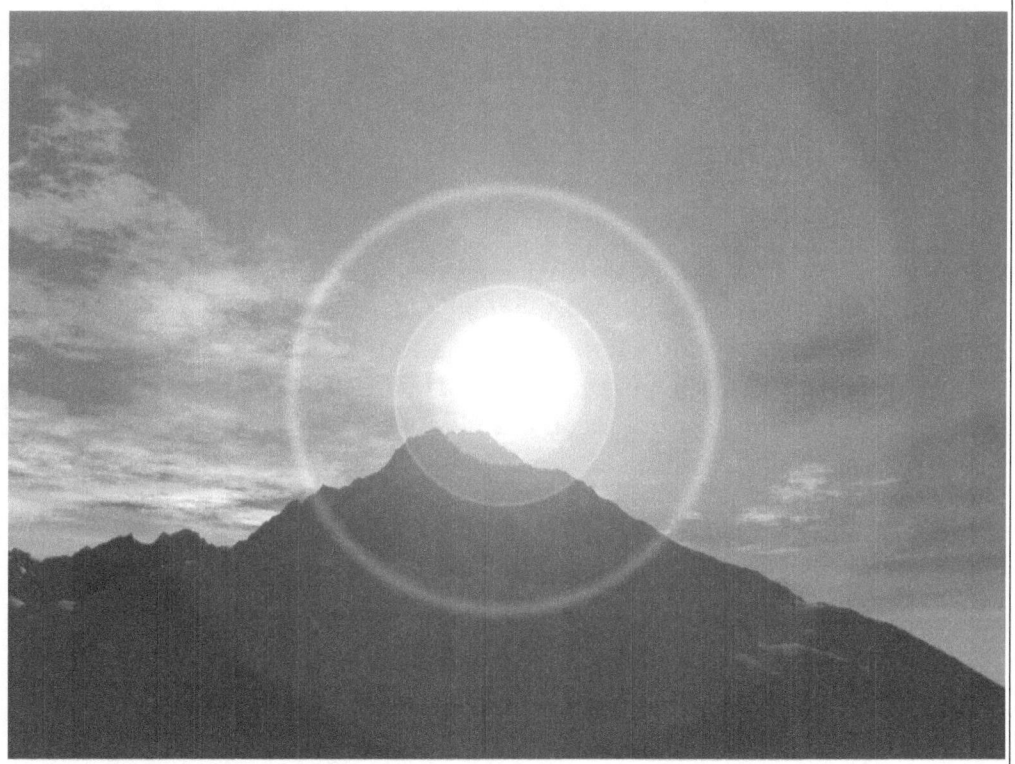

I BELIEVE

We all suffer to a greater or lesser degree
From the faults and failings of our parents.
Accepting our parents as flawed individuals
Is an important part of our growth
When confronting the reality of our own lives.

Final Note

Thank You

Without my wife Vicky, my life would not have soared. For with her I have walked hand-in-hand through trials, challenges and moments of serene perfection, and along the way discovered contentment and peace while laying my worms to rest.

My two children, Ayeesha and Bowie, each and every day bring warmth to my heart—a warmth and beauty which is so profound that to be without them is unimaginable.

It is because of the love and support of my family that I have been able to fulfil a dream and give to them and others a small part of the man I am today, and for that I will always remain grateful.

CONTENTS

Forward 5	Screams 82
	CREATION 83
SEARCHING 11	Crushed Violet Beds 85
Mighty Lady 13	Seduction 87
Monsoon At Sea 15	*WASTE* 89
Viking Gods 17	Lights of Dili 91
Warship Away 19	Listening 93
Lonely 21	*HIGHWAY* 95
REFLECTIONS 23	Gone 97
Lessons 25	Death Of A Boy 98
The Spark 28	Little White Mice Lost 100
DREAM 31	*ESCAPE* 101
Missing Home 33	Life Hurts 103
Eyes Of My Children 36	Live The Man 105
THOUGHT 39	*JEWEL* 107
Lost Thoughts 41	Heaven's Verandah 109
Worms 43	*FREEDOM* 113
The Politics Of Clown Phobia 44	Falling in Love 115
DISEASE 47	*CHANGE* 119
One Sip 49	Changes 121
Betrayal 50	Walls 123
Regret 52	*GROWTH* 125
TIME 55	Walk In The Rain 127
Age 57	A Social Gathering 129
Time 59	Coward 131
MUSIC 61	*HAZE* 133
My Passions 63	No Longer 135
My Love 65	Drunk With A Bar Girl 136
Scottish Rose 67	Liar 138
MINDS EYE 69	*BIRTH* 141
Faded Rose 71	Making Love 143
The Old Man's Stare 73	My Love For You 145
JADE 75	*DAWN* 147
Memory Lane 77	I Believe 149
So Warm 78	
HARMONY 79	*Final Note* 153
Growth 81	

www.ingramcontent.com/pod-product-compliance
Lightning Source LLC
Chambersburg PA
CBHW030646220526
45463CB00005B/1659